Once upon a team

exercises

CW01619453

Exercises to help members of teams (that's quite a lot of us!)

Michael and Maggie Kindred

Michael Kindred is a freelance games inventor and educational consultant. His hobby for many years became a full-time occupation in 1978. The main focus of his work now is the development of *4M Publications*.

Maggie Kindred is a senior lecturer in social work practice at Nottingham Trent University and a social worker for Nottingham City Social Services. Originally trained as a teacher, she moved into social work, where she has had a long career which has combined social work practice and training.

Michael and Maggie live in Southwell, Nottinghamshire and have a daughter, Cathy.

4M Publications

4M Publications

20 Dover Street, Southwell, Notts. NG25 0EZ
Tel/Ans/Fax: 01636 813674
e-mail: four.m.publications@btinternet.com

First published by 4M Publications 2001

P

Photocopiable

*In order to facilitate use of material in this workbook, please feel free to copy, photographically or otherwise, unlimited extracts. Permission is **not** given for copying the workbook in full, and copies of any parts of it are not for resale.*

ISBN 0 9530494 5 0

Further copies may be obtained from 4M Publications - see above for contact details

Printed by Roy Allen Print Ltd., Forest Road, New Ollerton, Newark, Notts. NG22 9PL

We would like to dedicate this book to writers, colleagues and students from whom we have learned a lot about being part of a team

Contents

Crises, hazards and obstacles 87

Introduction

Teamwork is group work but group work is not necessarily teamwork!

We have written this book because we believe that teamwork, which covers everything from a sports club to a family group, can be made more effective, enriching and fun by an understanding of its processes, and of the ingredients which distinguish teams from groups.

In order not to give rise to confusion, let's look at what *we* mean by the terms *group* and *team* as we are using them.

Similarities:

- Both involve people who get together for a purpose, not necessarily by choice, and who have something in common, eg a family is a group
- Both involve the skills, abilities, experiences, knowledge, values and attitudes of the people involved.

Differences:

- Teamwork involves a degree of interdependence. People who work together in the same room are not a team unless that have to *rely* on each other's contribution to get the job done

- Teamwork usually, but not always, involves some kind of hierarchy, eg a netball team has a captain, a team of volunteers has an organiser.

In thinking about these similarities and differences, consider the following: 1. All ducks are birds, but not all birds are ducks. 2. All teams are groups, but not all groups are teams. These statements can be illustrated by the following diagrams, (not to scale!) known in logic as Euler's circles, and in mathematics as Venn diagrams.

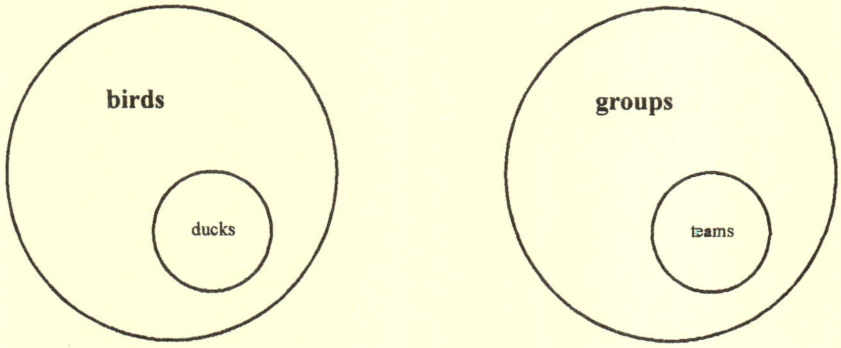

So, teamwork is group work, but group work is not necessarily teamwork.

In designing this book, we believe that:

- theoretical material should be pre-digested to meet the needs of busy people. The book is therefore a workbook, not a textbook, but it is grounded in theory. References are made in the text and a book list included. We have also given contact numbers and/or addresses for further information in some cases

- material should be photocopiable to make it readily accessible and practical for low cost group work. One workbook is therefore the only purchase necessary

- many modern workplaces are under heavy pressure and this results in people not 'looking after each other' even though they would like to do so. This book tries to find ways of redressing the balance

- teamwork takes many forms, from occasional contact to daily working together. This book is relevant to both: however its emphasis is on trying to help members deal with what happens when people are thrown together on a daily basis. So it is primarily a problem solving workbook. However, the experts on whom we rely come mostly from a humanistic school of thought: believing that positive change is possible and that human beings want to develop themselves. So we hope you will find an optimistic note throughout!

- teamwork should be fun - this reflects the philosophy behind all our books: learning should be fun

- you should take the issues seriously, but don't take yourself too seriously!

The exercises have been drawn from experience and the book is a product of the experiences, good and bad, which the authors have had in teams. Most of the exercises are original in that we have devised them ourselves. A few are our adaptations of standard themes. We have not knowingly plagiarised anyone else's ideas, but if you think that we have included anything too close to your own material for comfort, we should like to hear from you, so that the situation can be resolved to everyone's satisfaction.

Most of the theory comes from a white, western source, and needs to be modified to suit different cultures. Additionally, the race, gender, sexual orientation, state of physical ability and age of team members may affect the course of the exercises. It is important that you adapt them to your users every time.

In referencing our sources, we were unable to trace all the details of books and page numbers of some of the quotes. We decided, nevertheless, to include them as they seemed very important and too good to miss. Where possible we have acknowledged the respective authors.

It may be difficult to find the time for everyone in a team to take part in training and develment exercises, especially if the team is under pressure. Also, it may not be easy to con-nce the management of a firm or organisation of the benefits. It is worth stating the fun-mental principal on which this book is based: if the quality of the teamwork is improved, output from that team will also go up. You will only be able to demonstrate this point doing some of the exercises!

nally, this workbook may be used alongside *Developing Teamwork ... from an under-nding of personality,* (Goldsmith and Kindred, 2001). The two are different but comple-entary.

ase note that we have used the phrase 'group work' throughout, because as yet 'groupwork' is not a word that is any dictionary which we have consulted, though one of the authors has contacted Chambers about it to see if it can considered for inclusion in the next edition of their English Dictionary, as the word is used quite extensively now.

How to use this workbook

This workbook can be used to:

- **Understand** more about how teams work, what makes them tick and what can make them more effective
- **Assess** a team's ability and effectiveness
- **Develop** teamwork.

All the exercises are capable of being used independently. However, it is suggested that teams should use some of the assessment part (Where are you now?) first. This section is a mini team development course in itself. The exercises which follow have been put into the section to which they apply the most, but there is nothing rigid about this.

Where an exercise is particularly powerful, and may generate conflict, this has been noted at the beginning.

The times given for each exercise and debriefing are a guide only, unless otherwise stated, as people work at different speeds.

We have used the terms 'person/member/member of a team/team member/participant' interchangeably, as seems appropriate in the context.

A note on leadership

It is helpful, but not essential, to have someone to lead/facilitate the exercises. You may consider whether or not the person to do this is the actual team leader, eg: foreperson, organiser or manager. On the one hand, this could lead to discomfort, especially if there are some people in the team who don't get on very well with the leader. On the other, the actual team leader and/or the members of the team, may find it more difficult to work with an 'outsider' as a facilitator, and time is needed to develop the necessary relationship of trust. It may be that the use of an outside leader would be more beneficial if this workbook were used as a prolonged programme of team development.

However, the exercises are designed to be used by 'non-experts' in group work, as we believe that anyone can lead well if she/he has a sensitive manner and knows certain basic rules. We hope that the material leads to the conclusion:

> Of a good leader, when his task is finished, his goal achieved, they say 'we did it ourselves' (Lao-tse, in Jacques, 1984, p. 154).

Leadership essentials

- Read through 'Models of team life' (p. 10)
- Make sure that you know why the team needs the exercise in question each time you use it
- Look through the exercise(s) and the debriefing notes which accompany them, so that you are completely familiar with all that is involved
- Work through and apply 'Foundations of all group and team work' (p. 13) every time.

Some attention will need to be given to making the exercise work for you. Take the trouble to make sure everyone is comfortable, and if refreshments are to be offered, they are ones which people like. Different societies, age groups and people handle these 'housekeeping' things differently, so it is worth doing your preparation work very thoroughly.

Obviously you will not know 'where people are coming from' in every respect; what is important is to try to avoid assumptions. For example: asking people whether they are married assumes that they are heterosexual, as well as potentially exposing any recent bereavement or divorce. One of the authors hated this question when she was a single person who would have loved to be married. Times, arrangements and transport are all important. Ensuring that everyone is able to attend must be a priority.

Make sure that very important, though often 'invisible' team members such as caretakers and secretaries are considered. Who should attend is a matter for each team, but thinking about such issues is one of the most important aspects of the whole enterprise.

You can't play with half a team!

Other exercises suitable for team development may be found in ***Once upon a group exercises*** (See References). We suggest you consider the following:

1 Plaiting string; 12 Scapegoats; 18 The height of creativity; 26 Giving and receiving feedback

Models of team life

'To practise without theory is to sail an uncharted sea; theory without practice is not to set sail at all' (Susser 1968).*

Teamwork and group work are affected by the following, which operate at conscious and subconscious levels:

- the personality#, background, experiences, beliefs, attitudes, skills and abilities of each team member
- the relationships which exist and develop between members as the life of the team progresses
- the motivation which each individual brings to the team
- the extent to which the various levels of need of individual members of the team are being met.

There are various models and theories relating to the above. We reflected on and tried for fit many which helped us over the years. Those which spoke most to our experience were:

Maslow's (1943) hierarchy of human need
Schutz's (1958) group work model

We also draw on other authors and practitioners who have helped us over the years.

Maslow's hierarchy of human need

Maslow (1943), a member of the humanistic school of psychologists, said that there was a basic hierarchy of human needs as shown in the diagram on the right. His ideas represent a broad humanistic, or the putting of human concerns first, approach to understanding what makes individuals and groups tick, by looking at people's immediate needs and interests. The diagram has become famous for the distinctive way it is set out. We have taken the liberty of adapting it from the original for simplicity.

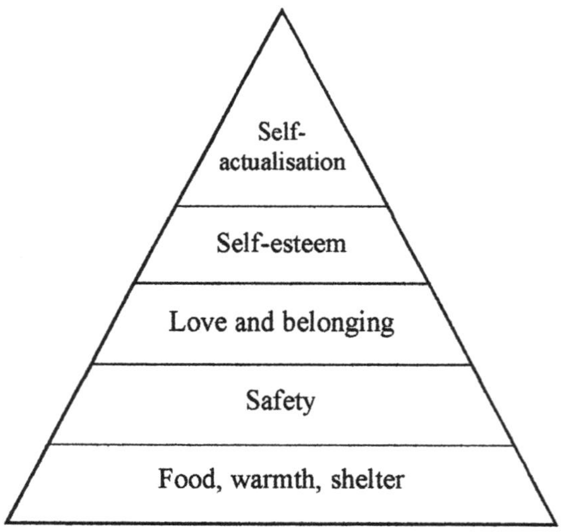

*The authors regret that no reference is available for this quotation.

#See ***Developing Teamwork ... from an understanding of personality***, (Goldsmith and Kindred, 2001).

Maslow also emphasises the potential for people to address and improve their own condition. He suggests that as the 'lower' needs are met, so people start to focus on the next level. It is difficult, if not impossible, to meet 'higher' level needs until the lower level needs have been satisfied, he postulates. Self-actualisation, a complicated term, will be explained in its context in the workbook. *We believe that this concept is important for team building.*

Schutz's group work model of Inclusion, Control and Affection

Schutz (1958), said that three basic phenomena are recognisable in all groups: Inclusion, Control and Affection. These form part of the building up process.

> Inclusion is concerned with thoughts and feelings about membership, belonging, acceptance, commitment, being and well being.
>
> Control centres around the question 'Who is in charge?' During the life of a group there will be many bids for control, and these are often, but not always, directed at the person who has been designated as leader.
>
> Affection is to do with the *creative bonds* which form between members, rather than *liking people.* These bonds help the group to enter its most productive stage, and make it effective and enjoyable.

The three phenomena also occur in the winding down process of a group, as its life draws near to a close.

> The bonds of Affection loosen first and are gradually dissolved. Members begin to be preoccupied with people and concerns outside the group.
>
> Members raise questions of 'Who is in charge?', 'What will happen now?'. These are Control elements.
>
> In the winding down of the Inclusion phase, members think about ending, leaving, loss, sense of achievement, sense of regret. The sense of Inclusion gradually dissipates.

These phenomena, Inclusion, Control and Affection continue to appear in varying proportions during the life of a group, even though at different stages one may seem more apparent than the other two. These three stages are never tidily completed and tensions are not necessarily wholly resolved. The process applies as much to a single meeting as to a whole series. For further development of these ideas, see Kindred and Kindred (1998a).

How does this model apply to the life of a team?

Inclusion:

Imagine that a new group of volunteers offers to clear a patch of wasteland to make it into a park. According to Schutz's theory, which corresponds with our observations, the volunteers will need to find their place by choosing what to do, staying near a friend for safety, asking for instructions, bringing tea and cakes to everyone, and all the other ways you will recognise as 'newness' in a group.

Control

Inevitably, we believe, following Schutz, members test out who is in charge, whether the designated leader or others. Rules are made and tested. This may be very comfortable, if based on members' knowledge, energy and choices, or uncomfortable, as in 'pecking order'. Control matters need to be satisfactorily resolved, but this does not mean that the designated leader imposes an iron regime. Rather it means that members are clear about what needs to be done, and what is negotiable and what is not.

Affection

It is important to recognise that in Schutz's terms, *affection* means *creative bonds*, rather than *liking people*, though this may be a by-product. For example, everyone in a club decides to bring food and drink for a celebration supper; if the teamwork is going well, there will be the right amount of sweet and savoury food with minimum fuss.

These creative bonds of affection lead to productivity and enjoyment if the control stage has been resolved satisfactorily. In a work situation, these bonds can and do exist, but sometimes are impeded by the nature of the heirarchical structure. If people are not reasonably satisfied by their task and relationships, 'productivity' will be affected.

Summing up

In trying to understand and develop a model of team life, we believe that:

- Human needs need to be satisfied for a team to work productively (Maslow)
- Team members need to feel included, to know where control lies, and to form creative bonds with others (Schutz)

The pages which follow reflect these beliefs. A team, like a life, is a journey. We have therefore divided the exercises into four sections, with 'signposts' for each. The final section, 'Celebrating Success' is shorter than the others - though the exercises are important and powerful - it's 'Getting There' which needs most of our energy.

Foundations of all group and team work

These include what are sometimes called ground rules, and like the foundation of a building they are fundamental to its continued existence. They are very basic - so how is it that they are so often ignored? We think that, behind such apparently obvious points, lie some issues which are not at all simple - making these links is what this workbook is about.

Ask yourself:

- **Is the place where the team fulfils its tasks accessible to all?**

  Are there any members with disability, either *evident*, eg persons in wheelchairs, or *hidden*, eg dyslexia or hearing impairment?

- **How is time-keeping dealt with?**

  This may not be the direct responsibility of the leader, as there may be a clocking-on machine, but the effects of any bad time-keeping can affect the relationships in the team. If it is the responsibility of the leader of the team, then he or she must deal effectively with anyone who is a poor time-keeper for the sake of those who are punctual, and for the organisation as a whole.

- **Is any aspect of the training or development work confidential?**

  If so, arrangements must be in place to deal with this, so that members of the team know what is for their ears only, and what may *never* be talked about outside the team. At one end of the spectrum, some workers have to sign the Official Secrets Act.

- **What feedback is allowed to other people outside the team?**

  This is not the same as confidentiality. The team may at times be working on something which, *for the time being*, needs to be kept within the team, so that it can be worked out properly. Alternatively, it may be necessary to pass information on. It needs to be clear to members exactly what will be disclosed.

- **Is the responsibility for different parts of the task, clear to all the members?**

If these responsibilities are not clear, there may be demarcation disputes which will affect the functioning of the team. It is a good idea for the leader to check from time to time that members still understand their responsibilities.

- **Is the place in which the team operates as conducive as possible to getting the tasks done?**

  In some buildings, the conditions can be very difficult. Some workers have to operate in extremes of heat, cold or noise, for example. It follows that caring about such things as temperature, lighting levels, ventilation, seating, pollution levels, and protective clothing, can help to improve the efficiency and motivation of each member of a team. Health and Safety Regulations will take care of some aspects of working conditions - but only if these regulations are implemented!

- **Is all equipment in proper working order?**

  Again, some of this concern will be covered by Health and Safety Regulations. It is important that members of the team feel free to notify the leader about any problems they notice to do with equipment - in some workplaces a person who is conscientious in reporting problems could be labelled as a trouble-maker.

- **How is smoking dealt with?**

  If your team is part of an organisation, there may already be a policy concerning smoking, so this question will not apply. The question which may then arise is how the smokers and non-smokers feel about it.

  If there is no policy in operation, it is worth checking out with members of the team how they feel about this, and whether or not they would like to initiate a policy.

- **How will the team cope with any absences which are not covered by medical certificates (ie: if a member keeps having odd days off for what appears to be no good reason)?**

  These kinds of absences can cause resentment among those members of the team who maintain a good attendance record. Are the absences saying anything about the way in which the team operates, the level of job satisfaction, the working conditions and so on, or is it something personal which is affecting the member's ability to attend regularly? If so, the sooner the situation is discussed with that person the better. The approach should avoid confrontation if possible so that the person feels free to air any grievances or problems.

- **Generally, do the attitudes of the members of the team convey messages:**

  - that reflect a positive view of black people?
  - that not everyone is slim, young and able-bodied? This includes being aware that there are hidden disabilities, eg not being able to travel in lifts.
  - that there are gay and lesbian people as well as heterosexuals?
  - which place women in an equal position with men?
  - that people are not to be discriminated against because of their age?
  - that people are not to be discriminated against because of any religious beliefs they may hold? This means being aware of religion when holidays are being allocated, for example.
  - that bullying and/or sexual intimidation are unacceptable?

- **If the members of the team are paid, is there any resentment about any differences in pay between members?**

  This issue comes high up the list of things which divide rather than unite! It may be that those responsible for the pay structure have a pay policy which is not negotiable, but awareness of how this can affect the motivation and morale of the team can help.

Signposts

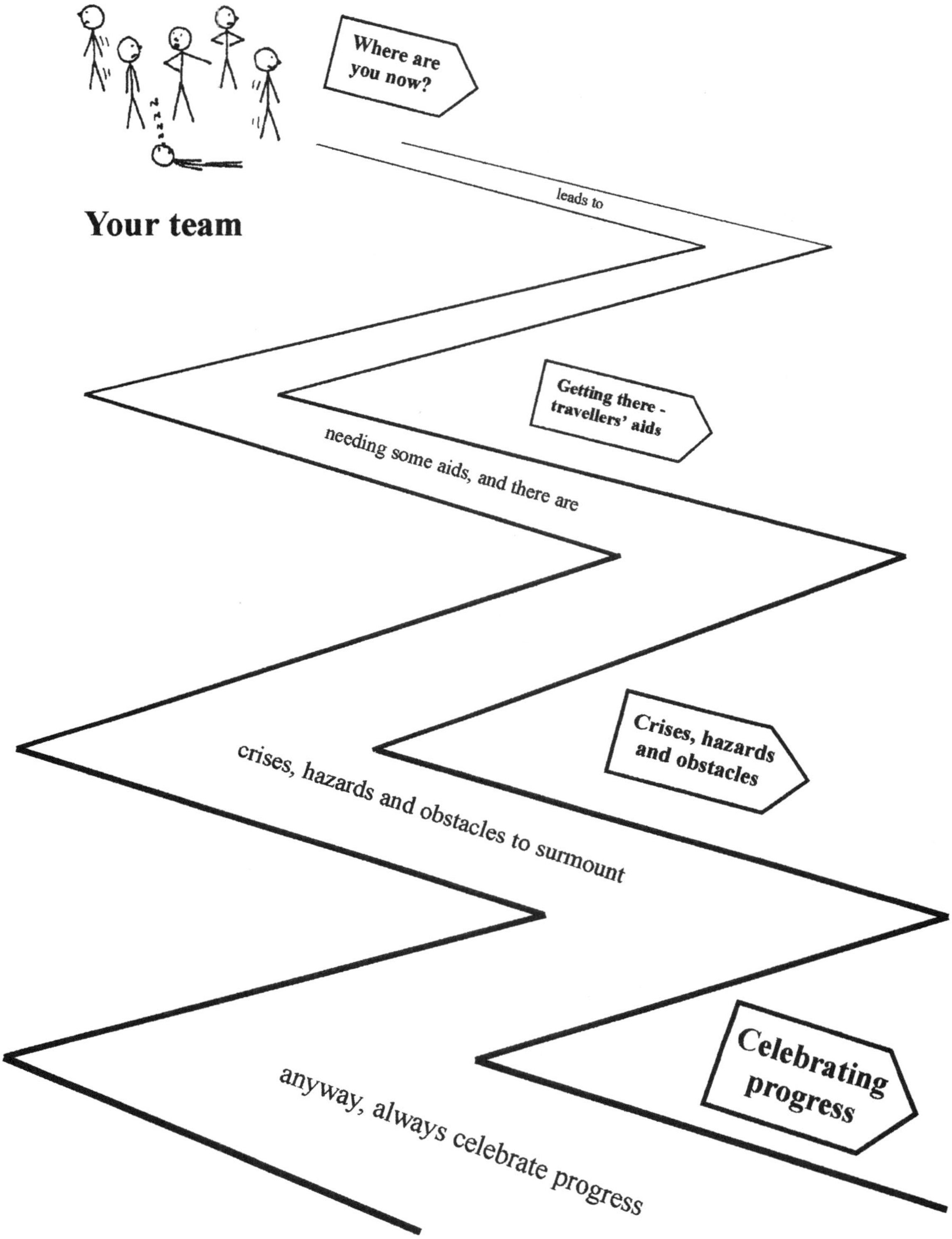

Your team
Where are you now?
leads to
Getting there - travellers' aids
needing some aids, and there are
Crises, hazards and obstacles
crises, hazards and obstacles to surmount
Celebrating progress
anyway, always celebrate progress

Where are you now?

A set of exercises for team assessment - overview

This section comprises seven exercises, 1, 2a, 2b, 3, 4a, 4b and 4c, to help the team assess its current position. The purpose and topics are listed for each one. The exercises could be used as a whole team development programme, and would need ample time. If, however, you have limited time available, please choose at least one topic from each exercise.

1

Purpose: To assess where the team is in relation to its aims and sense of purpose

- Aims generally
- What is most important to your team
- Sharing a sense of purpose
- Feeling that you 'own' your team
- Feeling committed to what you are doing

2a

Purpose: To assess where the team is in relation to working together

- Aids to getting where you want to be
- Guidelines to help things along
- Sorting out the jobs
- Making decisions
- Getting jobs done and nurturing each other
- Managing your time

2b

Purpose: To continue to assess where the team is in relation to working together

- Enough hands to do the job
- Conditions in which the team operates
- Sharing responsibility
- Sessions where you can talk things through
- Giving and receiving feedback
- Having regular reviews

3

Purpose: To assess where the team is in relation to the parts played by each member

- General things about playing your part
- Knowledge, skills, abilities, experience
- Everyone's part is part of all
- Joining in
- Being creative

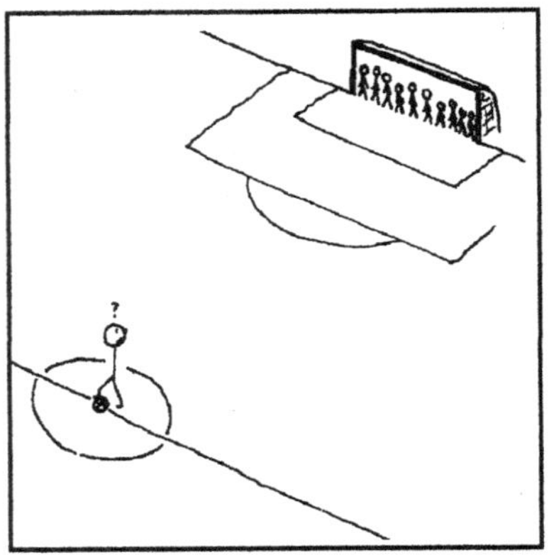

4a

Purpose: To assess where the team is in terms of its relationships

- Getting along with each other in general
- What makes your team tick
- Supporting each other
- Getting along with other teams/groups
- Being part of a wider picture

4b

Purpose: To continue to assess where the team is in terms of its relationships

- Communication
- Listening to each other
- Being sympathetic with each other
- Understanding the other person's position
- Being honest and trustworthy
- Having a sense of humour

4c

Purpose: To continue to assess where the team is in terms of its relationships

- Coping with stress
- Expressing feelings
- Dealing with conflict and confrontation
- Being optimistic and coping with pessimism
- Coping with success and failure
- Co-operating and coping with competition

Purpose: To assess where the team is:

- in relation to its aims and sense of purpose
- in relation to working together
- in relation to the parts played by each member
- in terms of its relationships

Time: Each exercise: about 20 mins
Each debriefing: about 1 hour

Materials: A photocopy of the Questionnaire for each person for whichever of the seven exercises you are going to use, a flip chart plus marker pens, a photocopy of the corresponding Action Sheets for each person, ready for the debriefing session.

Preparation: One week before the exercise takes place, give each team member a copy of the Questionnaire and ask them to fill it in without conferring with any other team members. Ask them to bring their completed copy to the teamwork session.

Exercise

On the flip chart collate the results for each question on the Questionnaire as follows:

1. Write the headings and questions on the left hand side, as on the Questionnaire, and make two columns on the right hand side, one for the 'smiling face', the other for the 'sad face'.

2. Record a) the responses to questions which do not have a 10 to 1 scale, and b) how many members put 'smiling faces' opposite each question, and how many put 'sad faces', writing the numbers in the appropriate columns.

Now: debrief the exercise using the accompanying notes as a guide.

Where are you now? Questionnaire for Exercise 1 (Sheet 1 of 2)

Purpose: to assess where the team is now in relation to its aims and sense of purpose
Please enter your response at the right hand side opposite each question. If there is a face at the right hand end, add a mouth to make it 'smiling' or 'sad' to correspond with your response.

smiling sad

Aims generally

What do you understand are the aims of your team at present?

To what extent do you think that members of the team understand the aims in the way in which you do?

A lot — Very little
10 9 8 7 6 5 4 3 2 1

What is most important to your team

List five things you think are most important to your team

1.
2.
3.
4.
5.

How far do you think members of the team agree on what is important?

A lot — Very little
10 9 8 7 6 5 4 3 2 1

How many different views do you think there are on what members think is most important?

Many — Very few
10 9 8 7 6 5 4 3 2 1

Purpose: to assess where the team is now in relation to its aims and sense of purpose
Please enter your response at the right hand side opposite each question. If there is a face at the right hand end, add a mouth to make it 'smiling' or 'sad' to correspond with your response.

smiling sad

Sharing a sense of purpose

To what extent do you experience your team as sharing a sense of purpose?	A lot ... Very little	10 9 8 7 6 5 4 3 2 1
How far do you think that some members are pulling in different directions?	A lot ... Very little	10 9 8 7 6 5 4 3 2 1

Feeling that you 'own' your team, in the sense of being generally in harmony with its aims and purpose

To what extent do you feel that you 'own' your team?	Very much ... Very little	10 9 8 7 6 5 4 3 2 1
How far do you think that some members feel 'out of it'?	Very much ... Very little	10 9 8 7 6 5 4 3 2 1

Feeling committed to what you are doing

How committed are you to the team purpose and tasks?	A lot ... Very little	10 9 8 7 6 5 4 3 2 1
How committed do you think the rest of the team are?	A lot ... Very little	10 9 8 7 6 5 4 3 2 1

Purpose: to assess where the team is now in relation to working together
Please enter your response at the right hand side opposite each question. If there is a face at the right hand end, add a mouth to make it 'smiling' or 'sad' to correspond with your response.

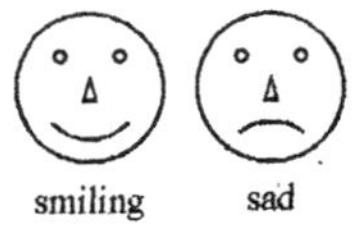

Aids to getting where you want to be

How good do you think the procedures are for getting where you want to be?

Very good									Very poor
10	9	8	7	6	5	4	3	2	1

Is the adminstrative help adequate? Don't evaluate the administrator(s) as a person(s): assess whether there are enough of them.

Guidelines to help things along

Do you think team members have enough guidance about how to do their job better? If you don't think so, please say what guidance you would like.

Sorting out the jobs

Do you think that the jobs are allocated fairly?

Are tasks prioritised by the leader and/or team members, or are they tackled in a haphazard way?

Where are you now? Questionnaire for Exercise 2a (Sheet 2 of 2)

Purpose: to assess where the team is now in relation to working together
Please enter your response at the right hand side opposite each question. If there is a face at the right hand end, add a mouth to make it 'smiling' or 'sad' to correspond with your response.

smiling sad

Making decisions

What decision making are you involved in, if any. Are you supposed to be?

Are you generally happy with the way in which decisions are made in the team?

Getting jobs done and nurturing each other

Is a balance achieved between attaining goals and being supportive of members?

Managing your time

How well do you think you manage your time in the team?

Very well — Not well
10 9 8 7 6 5 4 3 2 1

How well do you think team members manage their time in the team?

Very well — Not well
10 9 8 7 6 5 4 3 2 1

How well do you think the leadership/management regulates the demands on people's time?

Very well — Not well
10 9 8 7 6 5 4 3 2 1

Where are you now? Questionnaire for Exercise 2b (Sheet 1 of 2)

Purpose: to continue to assess where the team is now in relation to working together
Please enter your response at the right hand side opposite each question. If there is a face at the right hand end, add a mouth to make it 'smiling' or 'sad' to correspond with your response.

smiling sad

Enough hands to do the job

Do you think there are enough people in the team to do the job?

Do the aims and objectives need to be revised in the light of the resources available?

Conditions in which the team operates, such as the buildings, lighting, warmth and so on

How would you rate the conditions in which the team operates?

Very good — Very poor
10 9 8 7 6 5 4 3 2 1

Do you think the conditions are safe and healthy from both physical and mental points of view?

Sharing responsibility

Is there a feeling that everyone shares in the responsibility for the team's performance?

Sessions where you can talk things through

Are there any sessions available where you can talk to someone in a more senior position about any concerns that you have?

Purpose: to continue to assess where the team is now in relation to working together
Please enter your response at the right hand side opposite each question. If there is a face at the right hand end, add a mouth to make it 'smiling' or 'sad' to correspond with your response.

smiling sad

Giving and receiving feedback

Are there any systems in place which allow members of the team to give feedback to each other and the manager/leader about any aspect of the team and its work?

If so, is the feedback noted by the manager/leader, and is it acted upon?

Having regular reviews of what's going on

Are there regular reviews of how well the team is performing?

If so, how good do you consider the review procedure to be?

Very good									Very poor
10	9	8	7	6	5	4	3	2	1

Purpose: to assess where the team is now in relation to the parts played by each member

Please enter your response at the right hand side opposite each question. If there is a face at the right hand end, add a mouth to make it 'smiling' or 'sad' to correspond with your response.

smiling sad

General things about playing your part

	A lot									Very little
How much do you think the team benefits from the part you play	10	9	8	7	6	5	4	3	2	1

Knowledge, skills, abilities, experience

	A lot									Very little
To what extent are yours being used within the team?	10	9	8	7	6	5	4	3	2	1

Everyone's part is part of all

	A lot									Very little
How much do you think the part you play contributes to the whole team activity?	10	9	8	7	6	5	4	3	2	1

Joining in

	A lot									Very little
How well do you think team members participate in the various aspects of the functioning of the team?	10	9	8	7	6	5	4	3	2	1

Being creative

	A lot									Very little
To what extent can you be creative in the part you play in your team's activities?	10	9	8	7	6	5	4	3	2	1

Where are you now? Questionnaire for Exercise 4a (Sheet 1 of 2)

Purpose: to assess where the team is now in terms of its relationships

Please enter your response at the right hand side opposite each question. If there is a face at the right hand end, add a mouth to make it 'smiling' or 'sad' to correspond with your response.

smiling sad

Getting along with each other in general

How do you rate the quality of relationships between the members of your team?

Very good — Very poor

10 9 8 7 6 5 4 3 2 1

What makes your team tick

Is there a willingness to look at how members get on, or fail to get on, with each other?

Supporting each other

Do you feel that the team supports its members when they feel overwhelmed by pressure and stress?

Do you think that the team is a place for its members to feel safe from an emotional point of view?

How good are the strategies to support members through difficult times, either concerning personal problems or problems in the team or the umbrella organisation?

Very good — Very poor

10 9 8 7 6 5 4 3 2 1

Purpose: to assess where the team is now in terms of its relationships
Please enter your response at the right hand side opposite each question. If there is a face at the right hand end, add a mouth to make it 'smiling' or 'sad' to correspond with your response.

smiling sad

Getting along with other teams/groups

If your team has to work in collaboration with other teams either partly or wholly, are the relationships involved helpful ones?

To what extent is your team influenced by external factors?

A lot									Very little
10	9	8	7	6	5	4	3	2	1

Is it open to these?

Being part of a wider picture

If your team is part of an organisation, do you consider it *is* really part of that organisation, or is it a bit of an outsider?

If your team is part of an organisation, do you think other members consider it *is* really part of that organisation, or is it a bit of an outsider?

Where are you now? Questionnaire for Exercise 4b (Sheet 1 of 2)

Purpose: to continue to assess where the team is now in terms of its relationships
Please enter your response at the right hand side opposite each question. If there is a face at the right hand end, add a mouth to make it 'smiling' or 'sad' to correspond with your response.

smiling sad

Communication

How clear are the channels of communication between members of the team?

Very clear									Not clear
10	9	8	7	6	5	4	3	2	1

How clear are the channels of communication between your team and any other teams and /or management

Very clear									Not clear
10	9	8	7	6	5	4	3	2	1

How open, honest and friendly is the communication?

Very									Not very
10	9	8	7	6	5	4	3	2	1

Listening to each other

Do members listen to the views of other team members - do they really want to hear what is being said?

Do members feel free to respond when they have listened to what other members have to say?

Understanding the other person's position (being empathic with each other)

Do those who allocate the tasks have an empathic approach to those who have to perform them?

Where are you now? Questionnaire for Exercise 4b (Sheet 2 of 2)

Purpose: to continue to assess where the team is now in terms of its relationships
Please enter your response at the right hand side opposite each question. If there is a face at the right hand end, add a mouth to make it 'smiling' or 'sad' to correspond with your response.

smiling sad

Being sensitive to each other's needs

How sensitive are members of the team to each other's feelings and needs?

Very									Not very
10	9	8	7	6	5	4	3	2	1

Being honest and trustworthy

What is the level of trust between members of your team?

Very good									Very poor
10	9	8	7	6	5	4	3	2	1

What is the level of trust between your team and any other teams and /or those in management?

Very good									Very poor
10	9	8	7	6	5	4	3	2	1

Having a sense of humour

In general, do you think that members of the team have a sense of humour?

Purpose: to continue to assess where the team is now in terms of its relationships
Please enter your response at the right hand side opposite each question. If there is a face at the right hand end, add a mouth to make it 'smiling' or 'sad' to correspond with your response.

smiling sad

Coping with stress

How stressed are you within the team?

A lot									Very little
10	9	8	7	6	5	4	3	2	1

How stressed do you think others in the team are?

A lot									Very little
10	9	8	7	6	5	4	3	2	1

Expressing feelings

How easy or difficult does it seem to be to express feelings within the team, especially hostile ones such as anger, frustration and so on?

Easy									Difficult
10	9	8	7	6	5	4	3	2	1

Dealing with conflict and confrontation

How well do you think conflict and confrontation are handled within the team?

Very well									Very badly
10	9	8	7	6	5	4	3	2	1

Purpose: to continue to assess where the team is now in terms of its relationships
Please enter your response at the right hand side opposite each question. If there is a face at the right hand end, add a mouth to make it 'smiling' or 'sad' to correspond with your response.

smiling sad

Being optimistic and coping with pessimism

How optimistic do you feel about the team and its achievements?

Very ... Not very
10 9 8 7 6 5 4 3 2 1

How optimistic do you think the rest of the team feel?

Very ... Not very
10 9 8 7 6 5 4 3 2 1

Coping with success and failure

Do members of the team celebrate successes and help each other to cope with failures?

Co-operating and coping with competition

What level of co-operation between team members do you think there is?

High level ... Low level
10 9 8 7 6 5 4 3 2 1

How competitive do you think team members are with each other?

Very ... Not very
10 9 8 7 6 5 4 3 2 1

1. Discuss members' responses to the Questionnaire.

2. On the basis of counting the smiling and sad faces for each question:

   a) Smiles outweigh sads - congratulate yourselves. Have a general discussion about why members responded in the way they did.

   b) Smiles and sads roughly equal - discuss what lessons need to be learned.

   c) Sads outweigh smiles - these are the aspects which require some attention - discuss ways in which improvements could be made.

You may wish to have a break here, or re-convene later for the next part

3. Give a copy of the Action Sheets to each person. Explain that these are to guide each person's thoughts and that a master copy will be made during this part of the debriefing, with photocopies for each member afterwards.

4. Appoint one person to fill in the boxes on the collated team Action Sheet later (see 6 below).

5. Individually, think about and make notes on the Action Sheet. Ask people to write *only* what the team has control over.

6. Discuss responses to the Action Sheets and make a collated version. It will take time to agree on this. Make sure you decide on *who* and *when* for each action. If there isn't enough space, use plain paper, but keep the same format.

7. Give photocopies of the collated team Action Sheet to each member of the team. If necessary have a typed copy made first.

8. Fix times and dates for meetings at regular intervals to check on progress in putting the improvements into operation.

When the team have finished all seven exercises and debriefing sessions, congratulate them. They have done a very full and worthwhile 'diagnosis'

At the debriefing, one person will be asked to complete an Action Sheet as a master copy, and you will each be given a photocopy of it after the debriefing. This copy is for your own responses.

	Action		
	What	*Who*	*When*
Aims generally What needs to be done to make the team's aims clearer? List improvements which could be made to your team's aims.			
What is most important to your team List ways in which members can help each other to agree priorities.			
Sharing a sense of purpose What needs to be done to help team members feel more of a sense of shared purpose?			

At the debriefing, one person will be asked to complete an Action Sheet as a master copy, and you will each be given a photocopy of it after the debriefing. This copy is for your own responses.

	Action		
	What	*Who*	*When*
Feeling that you 'own' your team, in the sense of being generally in harmony with its aims and purpose What needs to be done to help members feel that they jointly 'own' the team?			
Feeling committed to what you are doing What needs to be done to develop members' sense of commitment to the team?			

At the debriefing, one person will be asked to complete an Action Sheet as a master copy, and you will each be given a photocopy of it after the debriefing. This copy is for your own responses.

	Action		
	What	*Who*	*When*
Aids to getting where you want to be generally What additional aids would you like to see introduced?			
Guidelines to help things along What additional guidelines would help things along?			
Sorting out the jobs In what ways would you like to see job allocation improved?			
What improvements would you like to see in the ways in which the 'batting order' of jobs is decided?			

At the debriefing, one person will be asked to complete an Action Sheet as a master copy, and you will each be given a photocopy of it after the debriefing. This copy is for your own responses.

	Action		
	What	*Who*	*When*
Making decisions In what ways could decision making be improved? In what ways could you all be more involved in decision making?			
Getting jobs done and nurturing each other In what ways could you achieve a better balance between getting the jobs done and nurturing each other?			
Managing your time In what ways could you manage your time better?			

At the debriefing, one person will be asked to complete an Action Sheet as a master copy, and you will each be given a photocopy of it after the debriefing. This copy is for your own responses.

	Action		
	What	*Who*	*When*
Enough hands to do the job If there aren't enough hands to do the job, in what ways could the situation be remedied?			
Conditions in which the team operates In what ways could these be improved?			
Sharing responsibility In what ways could members share more responsibility for the various aspects of what the team does?			

At the debriefing, one person will be asked to complete an Action Sheet as a master copy, and you will each be given a photocopy of it after the debriefing. This copy is for your own responses.

	Action		
	What	***Who***	***When***
Sessions where you can talk through things If these are not available, In what ways could they be set up? If they are, in what ways could they be improved?			
Giving and receiving feedback If these opportunities are not available, in what ways could they be set up? If they are, in what ways could these opportunities be improved?			
Having regular reviews of what's going on If these don't happen, in what ways could they be set up? If they do, in what ways could they be improved?			

Where are you now? *Action Sheet for Exercise 3* *(Sheet 1 of 2)*

At the debriefing, one person will be asked to complete an Action Sheet as a master copy, and you will each be given a photocopy of it after the debriefing. This copy is for your own responses.

	Action		
	What	*Who*	*When*
General things about playing your part How could you improve the way in which you contribute to the effectiveness of the team?			
Knowledge, skills, abilities, experience How could these be used to better advantage for the benefit of the team?			
Everyone's part is part of all How could all the team members be helped to feel that their contribution is valued as part of the whole?			

At the debriefing, one person will be asked to complete an Action Sheet as a master copy, and you will each be given a photocopy of it after the debriefing. This copy is for your own responses.

	Action		
	What	*Who*	*When*
Joining in In what ways could you be helped to join in more of the activities of the team?			
Being creative How could you be more creative in your contribution to the team's activities?			

At the debriefing, one person will be asked to complete an Action Sheet as a master copy, and you will each be given a photocopy of it after the debriefing. This copy is for your own responses.

	Action		
	What	*Who*	*When*
Getting along with each other in general In what ways could you all be helped to improve the way in which you get along with each other?			
What makes your team tick What training could you embark upon to learn more about the ways in which groups and teams work?			
Supporting each other In what ways could your support for each other be improved?			

At the debriefing, one person will be asked to complete an Action Sheet as a master copy, and you will each be given a photocopy of it after the debriefing. This copy is for your own responses.

	Action		
	What	***Who***	***When***
Getting along with other teams/groups In what ways can team members improve how they get along with other teams/groups?			
Being part of a wider picture If, as a team, you are feeling a bit isolated, what could you do to feel part of the wider world?			

At the debriefing, one person will be asked to complete an Action Sheet as a master copy, and you will each be given a photocopy of it after the debriefing. This copy is for your own responses.

	Action		
	What	*Who*	*When*
Communication In what ways could your communication with each other - eg face to face, e-mail, memo, phone - be improved?			
Listening to each other What could you do to make sure that colleagues know that you really want to hear what others say to you?			
Understanding the other person's position In what ways could you be more understanding of each other, and more caring about each other?			

At the debriefing, one person will be asked to complete an Action Sheet as a master copy, and you will each be given a photocopy of it after the debriefing. This copy is for your own responses.

	Action		
	What	*Who*	*When*
Being sensitive to each other's needs In what ways could you be more sensitive to each other's needs? **Being honest and trustworthy** This is a difficult one. Not many people like to feel that they are thought of as dishonest or untrustworthy. What thoughts have you which could help with this? **Having a sense of humour** How can you develop ways of laughing with each other, not at each other? How can you not take yourself too seriously?			

At the debriefing, one person will be asked to complete an Action Sheet as a master copy, and you will each be given a photocopy of it after the debriefing. This copy is for your own responses.

	Action		
	What	*Who*	*When*
Coping with stress In what ways could you help yourself and others to cope better with stress?			
Expressing feelings How could feelings be better expressed, so that they are not bottled up, or come out in inappropriate and perhaps hurtful ways?			
Dealing with conflict and confrontation Can you suggest some strategies which would help people to deal with situations where there is anger and differences of opinion?			

At the debriefing, one person will be asked to complete an Action Sheet as a master copy, and you will each be given a photocopy of it after the debriefing. This copy is for your own responses.

	Action		
	What	*Who*	*When*
Being optimistic and coping with pessimism How can you become more optimistic about the team and it's work? In what ways can you deal better with any pessimistic feelings? **Coping with success and failure** What ways could you suggest to celebrate successes? How could you cope better when things go wrong? **Co-operating and coping with competition** In what ways can you work more co-operatively? What do you think is helpful and unhelpful about competition?			

Getting there - travellers' aids

Exercises for team development

Getting there - travellers' aids

Human needs and teamwork 5

Purpose: To help the team meet basic human needs

Time: Exercise: 45 minutes
Debriefing: 30 minutes

Materials:
A4 size version of the 'hierarchy' diagram and a felt tip pen for each person. Flip chart and marker pen. (Blu-tack instead of marker pen if you decide to attach people's triangles to a flip chart sheets).

Preparation: Make an A4 sized version of this 'hierarchy' diagram for each person. It is important to have five sections in the triangle. Put a small number in each section as shown.

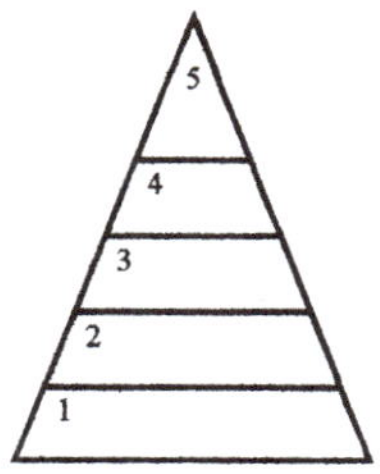

Exercise

1. Explain to the team that their motivation for the task in hand may depend on the satisfaction of basic needs which are very obvious but are often ignored.

2. Give out the triangle diagram and a felt tip pen to each person.

3. Ask each person to think about their everyday experience in the team. A helpful way of doing this is to think through the day from arrival to departure.

4. Using these recollections, ask each person to write the following in the wedge of the triangle indicated.

a) their experience of nourishment:

- are refreshments available?
- do people make drinks for each other?
- what do people do for lunch?

Record these responses in wedge 1 of the triangle.

b) Ask team members to think about the physical conditions in which they work:

- warmth/light
- amount of available space
- the security of the premises
- toilet facilities
- arrangements for anyone who has a physical disability
- safety

Record these responses in wedge 2 of the triangle.

c) Now go on to team members' feelings about the group. How far do people feel:

- valued by others
- supported in their work
- a sense of loyalty to the team

Record these responses in wedge 3 of the triangle.

d) Now consider the extent to which people feel that there is:

- a sense of purpose
- the possibility of developing and progressing in their work

Record these responses in wedge 4 of the triangle.

e) Finally, consider how far the following characteristics are present in self and others:

- acceptance of your own and others' foibles
- spontaneity
- creativity
- acceptance of reality without cynicism
- sense of humour
- job satisfaction

Record these responses in wedge 5 of the triangle.

5. Either: a) put all the triangles on a flip chart so that everyone can see them, **or**
b) spend time making a big triangle which incorporates everyone's words. This alternative will be essential if there are more than 6 - 8 people in the team.

Now debrief the exercise using the accompanying notes as a guide.

Maslow (1943) said that human beings operate by fulfilling basic needs as follows:

1. Physiological: hunger, thirst, bodily comforts
2. Safety and security
3. Belongingness and love
4. Esteem: achieve competence, gain approval and recognition
5. Self-actualisation: realising your full potential

The nub of this deceptively simple principle is that *human beings do not progress to higher levels in the hierarchy unless the lower levels have been met at least partially.*

This is obvious when considering starving people in a refugee camp, but is often overlooked in the sophisticated and complicated workplaces of the western world.

The team members may have recorded very little at the top of the triangle. If so, it is worth considering the very basic things at the bottom of the triangle. Without realising it, our energy can be used up in dealing with *apparently* unimportant details. If these are attended to, energy is thus released for the more satisfying and fulfilling aspects of team life. If you have recorded anything at the top of the triangle, celebrate!

Comment

As with all theories, you may already have observed that this one does not fit everyone. Some people will tolerate self-denial in order to satisfy needs further up the triangle.

However we think the model is helpful as it has a common sense logic which applies to most aspects of everyday life, where the exceptions only serve to prove the rule.

A refreshing break 6

Note: this exercise needs to be used after 'Human needs and teamwork', (p. 49), **to develop teamwork by using Maslow's principles.**

Purpose: To give team members a chance to respond to some of each other's basic needs, as defined by Maslow

Time: Exercise: 2 hours including preparation
Debriefing: 1 hour

Materials: Cups, saucers, plates, simple food such as biscuits and crisps, and drink. Be careful that you do not provide something that some-one cannot eat. An Exercise Preparation Sheet, similar to the one in the frame below, for each member of each mini-team.

Preparation: One week before this exercise, split the team into two mini-teams, of equal size if possible. Ideally, each group should be equally balanced, male and female, but as the composition of teams varies greatly, this may be impossible in some cases. Give each member of each mini-team an Exercise Preparation Sheet. The exercise itself would be best as an afternoon tea break. If it is not normal for your team to have such a break, treat this exercise as a 'one-off' experience.

A refreshing break: Exercise Preparation Sheet

Mini -team A comprises the following members: ***(Note to leader: enter team members' names here).***

The exercise takes place at ____am/pm on ___th _____ at ____***(Note to leader: enter time, date, place)***

Your mini-team will need to get together to plan the exercise.

In preparation you are to bring simple refreshments, eg drinks, biscuits and crisps, for the other half of your team. *Don't* prepare refreshments for your own half of the team. Plan out who is going to do what and when. You will have 15 minutes on the day immediately prior to the serving of the refreshments, to get them ready.

Mini-team B requires similar Exercise Preparation Sheets, but with the names of their members.

Exercise

NB: It is important to keep to time boundaries

1. Ask each mini team to appoint an observer who will take note of what happens between people in both mini teams during the exercise, which simulates a 'normal' refreshment break.

2. At the appropriate time, announce separately to each mini team, that they have 30 minutes to get the refreshments ready. After the refreshments have been consumed, the teams need time to clear away.

3. Announce separately to each mini team that a 15 minute refreshment break starts now.

Now: debrief the exercise using the accompanying notes as a guide.

1. Discuss the preparation stage:

a) Did team members know each other's requirements, eg diet, range of choice? How did they find these out?

b) How easy was this simple meal to organise? Our experience is that offering choice is a deceptively complicated matter. For example did each team provide enough of everything for everyone in the other team, thus risking quite a lot of waste, or did they find out who wanted what?

c) Ask members to be honest about the following aspects:

- was a vegetarian option serious - eg could vegetarians be sure that nothing contained animal fat?
- were all diets catered for, eg diabetic?
- were racial, cultural and religious options covered? For example Jewish people and Muslims would not appreciate being given crisps labelled 'bacon pieces' even if these are artificial flavours.

Our experience is that these matters, though not often discussed openly, generate a lot of heat. When organising training courses, for example, the authors find that it is sometimes a battle to ensure that there is enough tea, coffee and alternatives which do not contain caffeine. People's views about waste and indulgence come into play; it is perfectly true that choice generates waste, in catering terms. However, in a multi-cultural society, the hospitality rule is paramount, we believe.

2. How were the refreshments paid for? Again, the handling of petty cash can be an indicator of team health.

- do people pay willingly for their refreshments?
- are there team discussions about who pays for what, ie part-time members, the cost of different sorts of refreshments?

3. Reflect on 'small talk' during the break. You may argue that the fact that this was an exercise generated an artificial feeling. How different was it from normal breaks?

Consider how far the discussions were exclusive:

- talking about member's children may exclude those who do not have any.

- discussion about cricket and football *can* be gender biased!
- many conversations assume everyone is heterosexual.
  Example: 'What job does your husband do?'
- language is often thoughtlessly unkind, in the sense of not realising the impact. Example: when someone makes a remark about 'loonies' they may be making the person next to them who has a schizophrenic relative retreat further into a shell.

On the other hand, conversation may have been stimulating and enabling team members to understand each other better. Come to some conclusion about the general ability of your team to meet basic needs. Does any action need to be taken?

Some people may hate this exercise. Reflections about this will be interesting. However, as authors, we believe that the exercise illustrates Maslow's deceptively profound principle - basic needs are closely related to higher ones.

House rules 7

Purpose: To reflect on the unwritten rules within a team

Time: Exercise: 30 mins
Debriefing: 30 mins

Materials: Paper, pens

Preparation: None specific

Exercise

1. Appoint a leader. The following instructions are addressed to that leader.

2. Explain to the team that all families and teams develop a set of 'rules' which can be very powerful, even though people are often unaware of them and they are certainly not written down! As far as teams are concerned, make it clear these are *in addition* to the formal policies and rules!

3. Ask the team members to think about the way people behave during team time. Give examples of 'unwritten rules':

- In the family: Don't mention anything to do with sex when Mum's around.
- In the workplace: Never sit in the boss's chair in the office.

4. Now ask the team members to write down 'rules' which they think operate in the team.

Now: debrief the exercise using the accompanying notes as a guide.

1. Remind the team again that rules are powerful and that team members may like to discuss with a partner what they have written, before sharing with the whole team.

2. Collect a list of the team's unwritten rules.

3. Discuss how each rule came into being, and what, if anything, should be done about each one. Is it reasonable to have some unwritten rules in a team which are accepted and not questioned?

4. Discuss how many of the rules are positive?

Comment

'House rules' are an inevitable part of group life. Frequently they are useful: for example most people feel uncomfortable if they think they are wrongly dressed for an event. Others take pleasure in breaking the rules. What definitely causes distress is breaking rules which you did not know existed, a bit like swimming in a clear blue sea which has treacherous undercurrents. On the other hand, rules like bringing cake on someone's birthday are fun and enhance team life.

It may be helpful in understanding all this to refer to Transactional Analysis (Cryer, 1990). This theory suggests that all young individuals learn certain ways of feeling and behaving which become habitual when they are older - *'a life -script'.* One individual's script is very different from another's because of differences in how they were treated in early life by people they relied on and learnt from (Cryer 1990, p. 368). Individuals are seldom aware of their scripts because these scripts are so much part of them that that they do not normally consider examining them, and they might even have difficulty in teasing out what they are. So, house rules generally aim at making individuals more comfortable: sometimes this is at the expense of others. How far do your 'rules' enable people, or do some of them make some members seem more powerful than they really are?

We believe that bringing out some of these processes can result in a more satisfactory team performance. It takes time and patience to get to know people and feel comfortable with them.

Team Time 8

NB: This exercise is adapted from material in Goldsmith and Wharton (1993).

Purpose: To reflect on the team's use of time

Time: Exercise: 20 minutes
Debriefing: 30 minutes

Materials: Flip chart and marker pen.
Copy of Time Check sheet for each person.

Preparation: Make a copy for each person of the Time Check sheet on the following page.

Exercise

1. Nominate a leader, whose instructions are as follows:

a) Give each person a copy of the Time Check sheet and ask them to follow the instructions on it.

c) Now ask each person to add up their totals for the following sets of statements:

Set A: 1, 4, 9, 13, 18, 22
Set B: 3, 7, 12, 15, 21, 23
Set C: 5, 8, 11, 16, 20, 24
Set D: 2, 6, 10, 14, 17, 19

d) On a flip chart, write the names of the team members down the left hand side and put Set A, Set B, Set C and Set D as headings at the top, thus forming a grid. Ask each person for their totals for each set and enter them on the flip chart.

2. Put a ring round the highest total for each person.

Now: debrief the exercise using the accompanying notes as a guide

Time Check

For each statement, ring the number on the scale which you believe applies to you. **1** (the **No** end) indicates that a statement hardly applies at all and **10** (the **Yes** end) indicates that it applies very much to you.

	No									**Yes**
1. I am well organised	1	2	3	4	5	6	7	8	9	10
2. I think of time as something which can be made to fit the job	1	2	3	4	5	6	7	8	9	10
3. I always rise to the occasion	1	2	3	4	5	6	7	8	9	10
4. I'm realistic about getting things done in the time available	1	2	3	4	5	6	7	8	9	10
5. I like to spend as much time with people as they need	1	2	3	4	5	6	7	8	9	10
6. I spend a lot of time in planning in detail what I am going to do	1	2	3	4	5	6	7	8	9	10
7. I always deal with my letters, e-mails and phone calls quickly	1	2	3	4	5	6	7	8	9	10
8. I enjoy doing all sorts of leisure pursuits with other people	1	2	3	4	5	6	7	8	9	10
9. I find it easy to have a good clear out of things I don't need	1	2	3	4	5	6	7	8	9	10
10. I hate wasting time	1	2	3	4	5	6	7	8	9	10
11. I like to spend time thinking about the purpose of life	1	2	3	4	5	6	7	8	9	10
12. If there's a major crisis, I'm the one to deal with it	1	2	3	4	5	6	7	8	9	10
13. I like schedules to be adhered to	1	2	3	4	5	6	7	8	9	10
14. I can take it easy after thinking out how to tackle jobs	1	2	3	4	5	6	7	8	9	10
15. I love having my fingers in several pies	1	2	3	4	5	6	7	8	9	10
16. I always like to help people out, even if I'm very busy	1	2	3	4	5	6	7	8	9	10
17. Recreation and leisure pursuits are low on my priorities	1	2	3	4	5	6	7	8	9	10
18. I think taking responsibility for things is most important	1	2	3	4	5	6	7	8	9	10
19. I tend to forget about other people's most pressing needs	1	2	3	4	5	6	7	8	9	10
20. I feel guilty if I don't give enough time to the needs of others	1	2	3	4	5	6	7	8	9	10
21. I like to change my plans whenever necessary	1	2	3	4	5	6	7	8	9	10
22. I get fidgety if there's not a job to do	1	2	3	4	5	6	7	8	9	10
23. I can easily leave jobs until another day	1	2	3	4	5	6	7	8	9	10
24. I allow very little time to look after myself	1	2	3	4	5	6	7	8	9	10

When you have finished, the leader will ask you to add up the numbers you have ringed in each of four sets of statements, A, B, C and D. He will tell you which numbered statements are in which sets, and it might help to write the numbers in the spaces below:

Numbered statements in Set A: ___ ___ ___ ___ ___ ___ ___ Total for Set A: _____

Numbered statements in Set B: ___ ___ ___ ___ ___ ___ ___ Total for Set B: _____

Numbered statements in Set C: ___ ___ ___ ___ ___ ___ ___ Total for Set C: _____

Numbered statements in Set D: ___ ___ ___ ___ ___ ___ ___ Total for Set D: _____

Team time: *Debriefing* 8

Everyone talks about time, how there is too little or too much. Most people have their own views on priorities to do with the use of time.

Its use may not be so rational as we think, ie it may have more to do with personality, according to Hirsh(1985). She used a personality theory by Myers-Briggs* which offers useful pointers to the team use of time. The scores may now be interpreted in the light of these pointers:

Set A: The higher your score is above 33, the more likely you are, according to Myers Briggs, to 'warm to structures and hierarchies, and believe that it is important to earn your place and do the right things at the right time'. The lower your score below 33, the less likely that this is the case.

Set B: The higher your score is above 33, the more likely you are to, according to Goldsmith and Wharton (1993, pp. 78ff), be 'happiest when dealing with concrete problems', realistic, shying away from the theoretical, liking variety, and full of fun.

Set C: There are fewer of this type in society, according to Goldsmith and Wharton (1993, p. 83). The higher your score above 33, the more you will 'have a shared concern, perhaps passion would be a better word, for competence - you like to do things well whatever the circumstances'.

Set D: The higher your score is above 33, the more likely you are to look at any situation and see the possibilities, according to Goldsmith and Wharton (1993, pp 83-84). You eat, sleep and breathe people. You dislike conflict and may find it hard to understand why everyone is not caught up in a search for meaning, as they are.

As a team, make a note of the people who are *predominantly* each type, and see how far the team has a balanced spread of personality types. If it has, you *may* have less arguments, but a narrower use of possibilities. What action needs to be taken, if any?

For a much more detailed description of the personality types outlined above, see Goldsmith and Wharton (1993), and for a guide to how teamwork may be interpreted in the light of them, see Goldsmith and Kindred (2001).

**Myers-Briggs Type Indicator*™ and MBTI™ are trademarks of Consulting Psychologists Press, Inc.

The power tree 9

Important: this is an exercise which may raise strong feelings, so plenty of time should be allowed for debriefing

Purpose: To recognise how power is seen and used in a team

Time: Exercise: 15 minutes
Debriefing: 1 hour

Materials: A copy of the Power Tree (next page) for each person. A large version of the Power Tree drawn on flip chart paper. Flip chart, pens and marker pens.

Preparation: Photocopy enough copies of the Power Tree (next page) for each person. Draw a large version of the Power Tree on a piece of flip chart paper.

NB: Using the individual sheets makes it more private for people. Using the large piece of paper afterwards has the virtue that everyone is able to see the pattern which emerges.

Exercise

1 Explain to the team that power is a complicated concept and the people who are the designated leaders are not always the most powerful. For example: there is power in being the boss, but there is also power in being a man rather than a woman, able-bodied rather than disabled.

2 Ask team members to think about the way they feel in relation to others.

3a. Ask each person in turn to draw themselves somewhere on the Power Tree to show how they *feel* in relation to other people in the team and put their initials next to the drawing. Explain that the top part of the tree is the most powerful.

3b. Now ask each person in turn to draw the others in the team where they *feel* they are in relation to themselves and each other.

4 Ask each person in turn to comment on *either* the team picture which has emerged, *or* their individual tree, which they may wish to place in the middle of the circle for inspection

5 Discuss the different views and perceptions which emerge.

Now debrief the exercise using the notes overleaf as a guide.

Power Tree

1. Draw yourself somewhere on the Power Tree to show how you *feel* in relation to other people in the team, the top part being the most powerful.

2. Draw the others in the team where you *feel* they are in relation to you and each other.

In both 1 and 2, this may or may not be related to your position in the team, eg the leader or boss may feel themselves to be powerless.

It may be helpful to start by recognising the fact that all teams, from the highest-powered corporation to the most informal of organisations trying to improve the appearance of their town or village, depend on the use of power.

Secondly power in itself is not wrong, it is a necessary part of life. A young child cannot have power equal to that of an adult. It is the *misuse* of power, or oppression, which is unacceptable. Part of your forthcoming discussion may be about whether people with more training or experience should have more power. Before doing this it is worth looking at what Hunt (1979) calls 'the drama of power', which is normal, human and not indicative of an unhealthy team.

Now share as much as you want of your 'power tree'. In order to ensure that your discussion stays constructive, it may be helpful to keep referring to the following:

- Structure is essential for efficient working - leaders cannot always be popular, and it may seem at times that the structure is more important than the people.

- Do not be afraid to experiment. However, check the nature and frequency of experiments. It is well documented that too many re-organisations sap employee morale, for example, the constant reorganisation of Local Authority bodies.

- Negotiation is essential. The smallest change needs to be announced, discussed and the reason for it explained, if it is non-negotiable.

- 'People who want power have the potential to use it well'. This is a dangerous generalisation, but we can all think of people who have had power thrust upon them, perhaps for career reasons or for financial gain, who have struggled and who have wished that they had not achieved it. If this applies, remember that you *have* got the potential to develop.

- The above applies to *everyone*. The person who has the key for a particular cupboard is very powerful and has it within his/her grasp to stop productivity for a day.

- The fact that there are sub-groups is normal, according to Turkie (1995)*.

*The authors regret that no reference is available.

> Accept the right of sub-groups to form and have a separate life, especially in a large organisation. These often mirror the wider society, ie black people, gay and lesbian members, women and disabled people may wish to gather for support. These are not a threat to the organisation and may enhance it by bringing ideas which may not have been thought of.
> A sub-group is not necessarily a clique.
>
> - Power and conflict can bring energy, if this can be discussed openly, and directed constructively.

Comment

This is our version of a standard exercise - it illustrates the point that in human relations, things are not always what they seem. Did you find that someone who apparently has quite a small role in a team may be amazed to find themselves perceived as very powerful. Such power may be seen as either negative or positive. If the exercise has brought up very strong feelings, it may be necessary to have another session about it. 'Vertical Slice' (p. 65) may be useful.

> I sometimes think that 99 per cent of suffering has to do with how devalued people feel by the labels put on them or the derogatory opinions they hold about themselves (Hoffman 1993, p. 79).

How often have you heard someone saying they are 'just the receptionist'. It may be helpful here to make a distinction between *influence* which you can have whatever your role, and *power*, which is bestowed on you by your role, eg parents, bosses and leaders all have power. Children, employees and group members can and do have a very strong influence.

Vertical slice 10

Important: This exercise is for team members and the leader(s)/ manager(s) together, and is a powerful exercise which could generate strong feelings

Purpose: To develop trust and co-operation between team leaders and members

Time: Exercise: 30 minutes
Debriefing: 30 minutes

Materials: Pens and paper

Preparation: None specific

Exercise

1. Give out pen and paper to each person.

2. Ask the leader (it may be you) to write down the following as if in a non-leadership role in the team:

   a) what they think needs to change in order for the team to function better
   b) what existing good qualities they would like the team to develop

3. Ask those who are in a non-leadership role to write down the following:

   a) what they would like the leader to do to help the team to function better
   b) what existing good qualities they would like the leader to develop

4. Ask each member in turn to choose the most important thing they want to share, from what they have written, so that the team can discuss it.

5. Make a list of the suggestions which the team could adopt.

6. Discuss the different ways of looking at the same team.

Now: debrief the exercise using the accompanying notes as a guide.

We hope this exercise gave you the opportunity to look at the team from what often seems the opposite side of a yawning chasm between leader and members - a 'vertical slice'. In reality, how far was there common ground in your team? Alderson (1992)* summarised the essence of good teamwork as follows:

- good interpersonal relationships with understanding of each other's values
- the ability to discuss openly without arousing undue sensitivity or tension
- a high level of trust in each other
- to be approachable and able to accept feedback and criticism, developing the ability to give and receive feedback in a non personal and objective manner
- sufficient discipline and cohesion to implement decisions upon which they agreed
- the capacity to discuss long and short term issues

The chances are that your aspirations for the team, either as leader or member, went something like the above. If not, we suggest Exercise 16 - 'Moving the roadblock'.

Comment

If you have found this exercise demanding, or are wondering whether it has done more harm than good, the following from the National Institute for Social Work (NISW), may help:

> Resolving conflict increases security about the team's coping ability. Unresolved conflict is hazardous ..... resentment and ill-feeling may grow into disunity and disaffection (NISW 1996, p. 4).
>
> A happy team will not of itself produce excellent work. There must be standards, targets and performance indicators (NISW 1996, p. 4).

Finally, can you afford to ignore problems?

*The authors regret that no reference is available for this quotation.

The envelope factory 11

Purpose: To develop teamwork skills by setting up a 'production line'

Time: Exercise: 30 mins
Debriefing: 30 mins

Materials: 20 sheets of A4 paper. 2 each of the following: pencil, ruler, rubber, pair of scissors, Pritt stick.

Preparation: Make two photocopies of the instruction sheet on the following page. In one corner of the room put a table and five chairs, and do the same in the opposite diagonal corner.

Some teams could be a little over-ambitious!

Exercise

1. Form two teams of five. Any remaining participants should act as observers.

2. Tell each team that they will receive instructions for making some items.

3. Tell each team to go to a table.

4. Give each team an instruction sheet.

Now: debrief the exercise using the accompanying notes as a guide.

Instruction Sheet

Starting now, you must organise yourselves as a team to make 10 envelopes as per the diagram below, which must be reproduced full size on each A4 sheet. The pieces marked 'X' are to be cut off. The flap which closes on each envelope does not require to be gummed! As a team, you must decide how best to set up the production line. The time stops when one team has finished, or when 30 minutes is up, whichever is the sooner. The leader of this exercise will act as the Quality Control Officer for both teams.

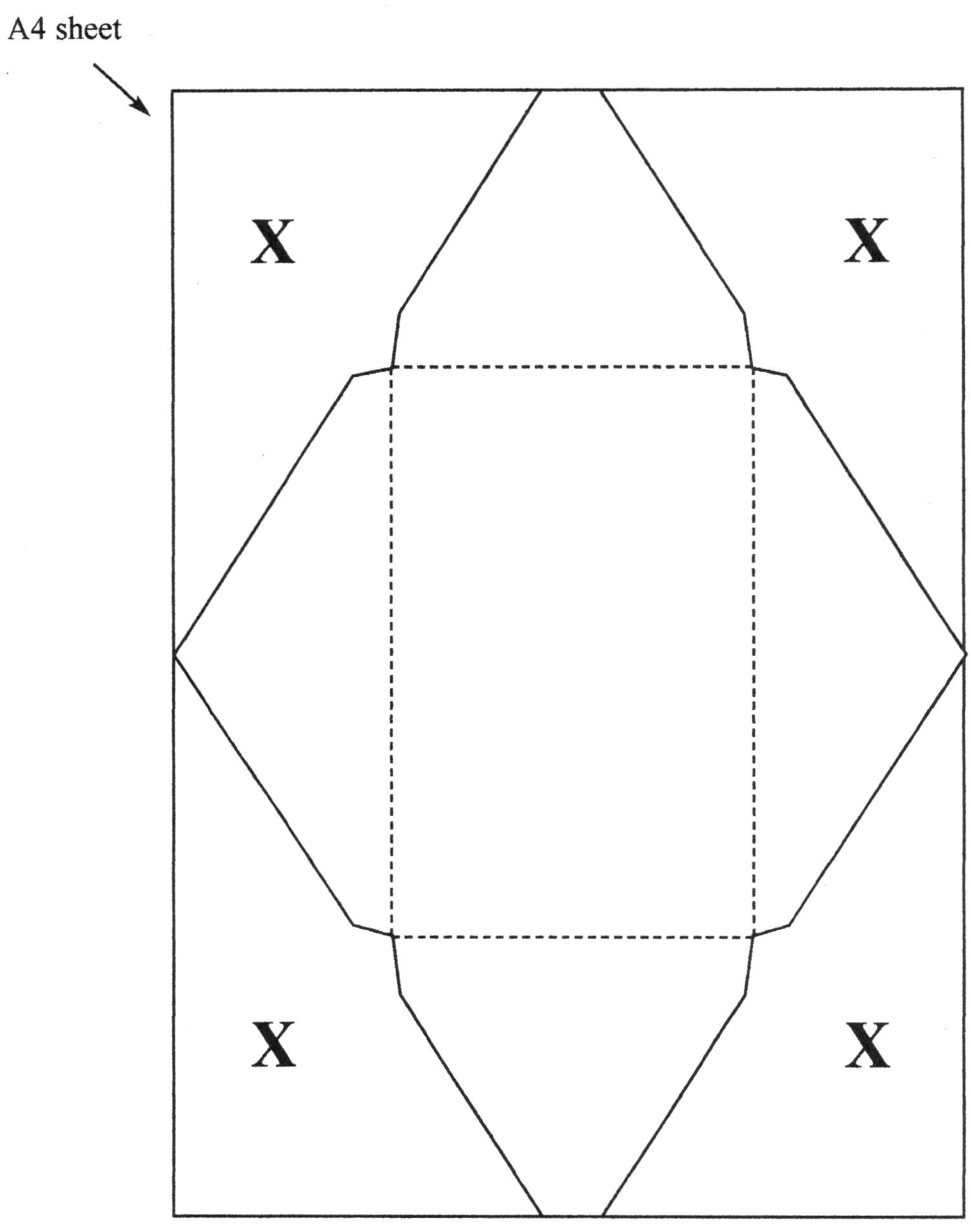

Scale: Half full size Dotted line = a fold

1. First of all, do a quality control check on the envelopes for each team and give each completed envelope a mark out of 5.

2. Add the total marks for each team.

3. Now ask each team in turn how they set about tackling the exercise. Use the following as a prompt list:
   a) was a team leader appointed, and if so, how?
   b) who was involved in deciding how the production line should be set up?
   c) what kind of production procedure was adopted - did each member individually produce a complete envelope, or did one member do all the drawing, one the cutting out, and so on?
   d) if the latter in 'c' above, how were the jobs allocated?
   e) what thoughts and feelings were around:
      - at the start of the exercise, once team members knew what they had to do?
      - during the exercise?
      - when they had finished?
   f) were any of the following present: enjoyment, panic, a sense of fulfilment, resentment about anything, a feeling of being manipulated.

4. If this exercise was used in a work-based team, were there any parallels with their actual work situation? For example, did participants experience any frustration over lack of resources - would they have liked more scissors, pencils?

5. What does the team need to do differently when tackling a common task?

Comment

Some people do not like 'simulations'. There is much discussion in learned journals about their effectiveness. 'Regardless of gender, young children enjoy play activities ..... after the age of twelve girls become less interested in games ..... boys value team participation and competition (Baranich 1992, p. 159). Does this ring any bells for your attitude to the simulation?

Getting to know you **12**

Purpose: To help team members to get to know each other better, by learning something about their 'out-of-team' skills

Time: Exercise: 5 mins x number of people in the team
Debriefing: 45 mins

Materials: A copy of the Job Sheet for each person. Pens or pencils. Flip chart and marker pens.

Preparation: Make sufficient photocopies of the Job Sheet (see next page).

Exercise

1. Give each person a Job Sheet and ask them to follow the instructions on it.

2. Now choose one of the participants and ask each of the other participants in turn to say what job they had chosen for them, and put the results on the flip chart.

3. Repeat the procedure with each of the other participants in turn.

Now: debrief the exercise using the accompanying notes as a guide.

Job Sheet: Instructions

1 Look through the list of jobs below, decide which job you would be most interested in doing and put a tick in the square at the left hand side of it.

2 Make a list of the names of the other participants in this exercise in the spaces at the top of the table. In the column under the name of the first person, put a tick against the job you think they would be most suited to them. Use your knowledge and experience of them to help you do this. Repeat the procedure for each participant.

3 Await further instructions from the leader of this exercise.

		Write participants names in the boxes immediately below											
Your choice	**Job description**												
	1. Fix a shelf to a wall including drilling the wall and fixing the brackets												
	2. Knit a sweater												
	3. Shop at a supermarket for provisions for a family of four for a month												
	4. Dress a child's deep wound and take her/him to the doctor for a tetanus injection												
	5. Play tennis from a wheelchair												
	6. Move three large deeply-rooted shrubs from one part of a garden to another												
	7. Write a letter to a friend who has just suffered a painful bereavement												
	8. Teach someone how to use a computer												
	9. Clean the car inside and out												

1. Choose a participant and ask them to divulge what job they chose for themselves, and check this against the results from the team. Were there any surprises? Ask for general comments about the evidence on which people made their assumptions.

2. Repeat the procedure for each of the participants in turn.

3. Discuss the results and evidence, or lack of it, generally. The following may help to inform the discussion.

Starting from the moment we first become aware of another person, we make assumptions about them, consciously or unconsciously. The awareness may arise from a face to face meeting, a phone call, a letter, an e-mail, or we may have heard them on the radio or seen them on TV. Quite often we base these assumptions on little or no evidence, and so they may stem, for example, from our intuition or prejudices. For example, we may see someone on TV for the first time and assume that they are a certain kind of person, and some evidence may come to us later on which contradicts or confirms our assumption.

These assumptions can determine to some extent how we behave towards a person, how we relate to them and how we respond to them. If the assumptions are wrong because we have not bothered to base them on hard evidence, then our behaviour, relationship and responses may be inappropriate. Imagine how this could affect the functioning of a team of 10 people in which there are 45 different relationships going on! (for formula see Kindred and Kindred 1998a, p. 10).

Comment

'An adult is what he has done' (Knowles, 1983, p. 61). Note that Knowles still uses sexist language - we have left it to preserve the authenticity of the quotation! Educators over the years have recognised that people learn and develop quicker and more creatively if they build on their existing experience. *This means all their experience,* not just the task in hand, a fact sometimes overlooked in the pressure to get the job done. Women often define themselves as 'just housewives' and those in low paid or low status jobs as 'just labourers/cleaners/drivers'. The authors believe that the more people's total experience and talents are recognised, the better they will perform. We hope that the spin-off from this exercise may also be that you have found out a whole range of abilities that will come in useful!

A piece of cake! 13

NB: you will need at least 8 people

Purpose: To explore co-operation in the team

Time: Exercise: *10 mins maximum*
Debriefing: 30 mins

Materials/equipment: 1 set of eight 'pieces of cake' (as described below in Preparation).
A circular table about 75cm (2'6") diameter (best) or one about 75cm square would do.

Preparation (of the 'pieces of cake)**:** See instructions on each of the next four pages.
NB. The process of plate-making, printing and your photocopying may result in slight distortion of our original drawings. If the pieces don't quite fit, trim a little bit off the edge of one to ensure a fit.

Exercise

1. If you have more than eight people, choose 8 and ask the rest to act as observers.

2. Give each of the eight people a 'piece of cake', *numbered side down,* and tell them to keep it that way up during the exercise and not to look at the number on the other side.

3. Explain that each piece has two v-projections on one side and 3 v-slots on the other. The two v-projections on one side of a piece fit into two of the three v-slots on the side of another piece.

4. Ask each person to keep hold of their piece of cake, *numbered side down,* at all times during the exercise, and work with the other participants in trying to fit all eight pieces together to form a 'cake'. Explain that they have a maximum of 10 minutes from when you say 'start', and that you will notify them when the time is up. Also explain that if they solve the puzzle within 10 minutes, you will re-allocate the pieces, and that they are to try again.

Note for the leader: There is only one way in which the pieces will fit together to form a complete circle – or cake, but there are many ways in which the pieces will almost fit together, but the final 1 or 2 pieces won't fit, hence the puzzle has a frustration factor!

Now: debrief the exercise using the accompanying notes as a guide.

The 'Piece of cake' is adapted from the Tour of Knowledge idea devised by Michael Kindred and Malcolm Goldsmith. The idea was patented and marketed as Quiz Cards by Waddingtons Playing Card Co Ltd.

A piece of cake: Diagram Sheet 1 of 4

1. Photocopy this Diagram Sheet
2. Paste it onto stiff card.
3. Preferably using a cutting knife and a metal straight edge (one which is guarded to protect fingers - if you haven't got one of these - be careful!), cut out the two shapes as accurately as possible. Scissors may be used on thinner card, but the cutting may be less accurate.
4. Solve the puzzle yourself by fitting the pieces together to check that they fit properly.
If necessary, refer to the solution on the debriefing page!

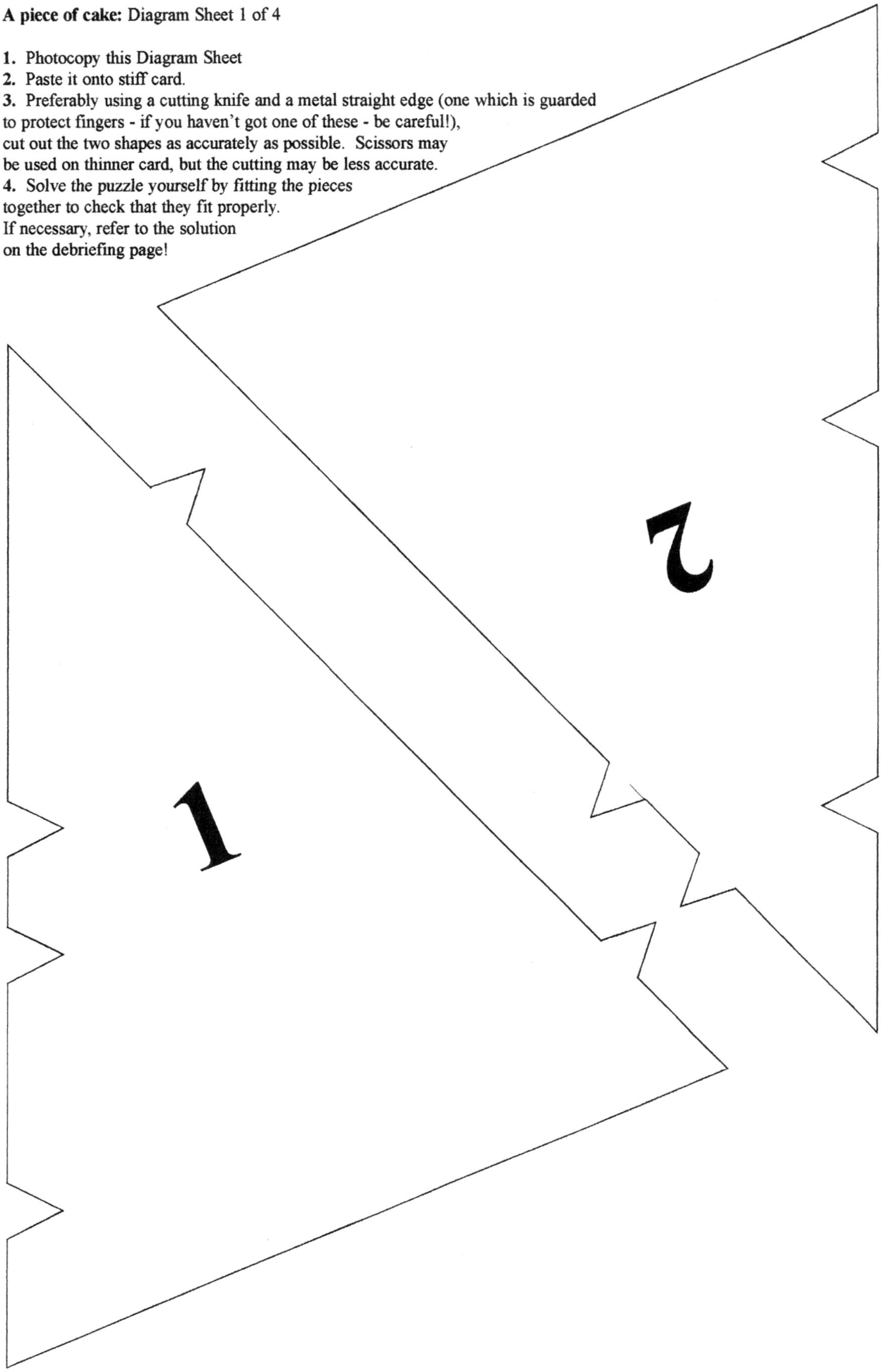

A piece of cake: Diagram Sheet 2 of 4

1. Photocopy this Diagram Sheet
2. Paste it onto stiff card.
3. Preferably using a cutting knife and a metal straight edge (one which is guarded to protect fingers - if you haven't got one of these - be careful!), cut out the two shapes as accurately as possible. Scissors may be used on thinner card, but the cutting may be less accurate.
4. Solve the puzzle yourself by fitting the pieces together to check that they fit properly. If necessary, refer to the solution on the debriefing page!

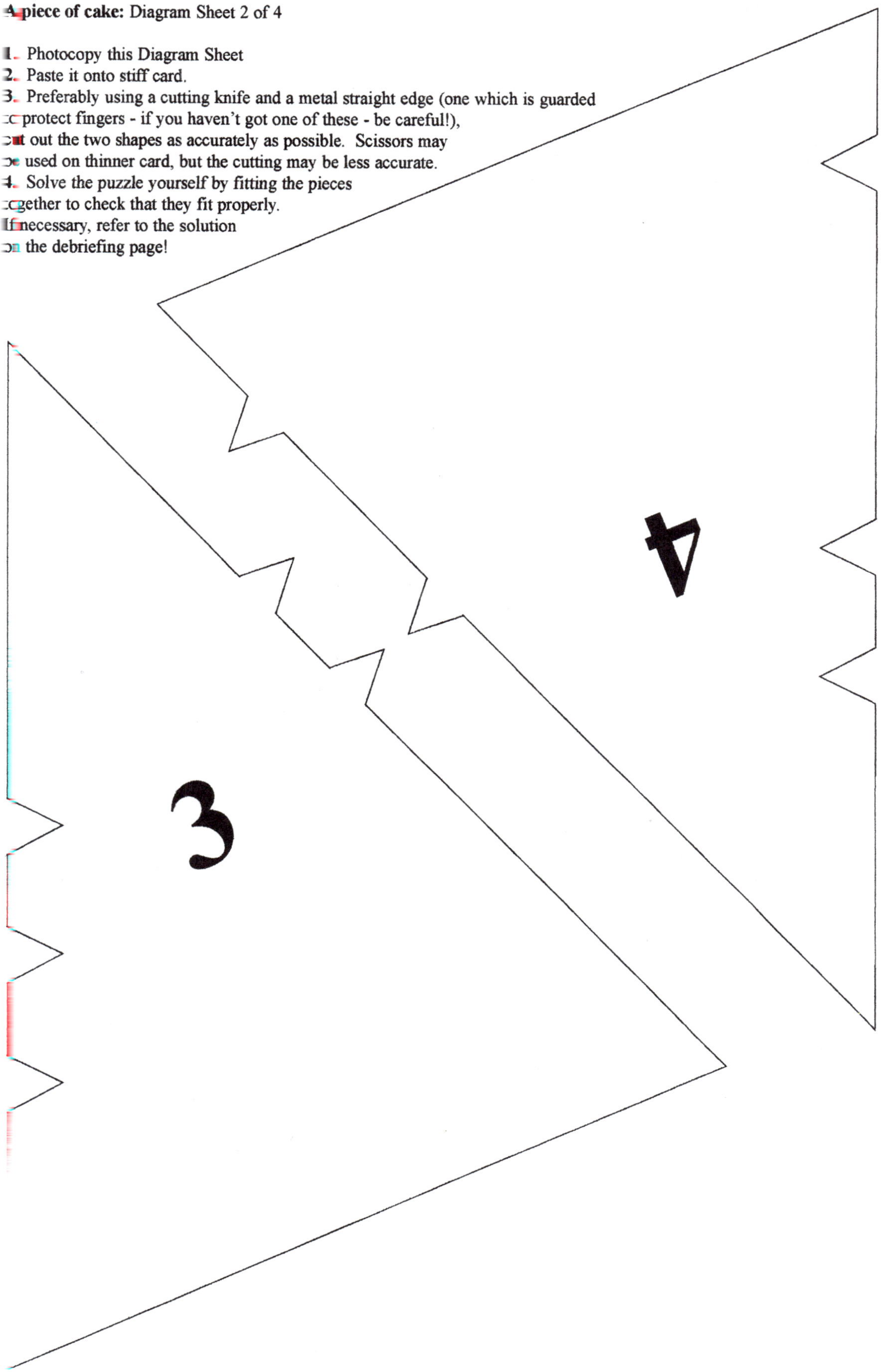

A piece of cake: Diagram Sheet 3 of 4

1. Photocopy this Diagram Sheet
2. Paste it onto stiff card.
3. Preferably using a cutting knife and a metal straight edge (one which is guarded to protect fingers - if you haven't got one of these - be careful!), cut out the two shapes as accurately as possible. Scissors may be used on thinner card, but the cutting may be less accurate.
4. Solve the puzzle yourself by fitting the pieces together to check that they fit properly.
If necessary, refer to the solution on the debriefing page!

A piece of cake: Diagram Sheet 4 of 4

1. Photocopy this Diagram Sheet
2. Paste it onto stiff card.
3. Preferably using a cutting knife and a metal straight edge (one which is guarded to protect fingers - if you haven't got one of these - be careful!), cut out the two shapes as accurately as possible. Scissors may be used on thinner card, but the cutting may be less accurate.
4. Solve the puzzle yourself by fitting the pieces together to check that they fit properly. If necessary, refer to the solution on the debriefing page!

A piece of cake!: *Debriefing*

Sometimes, as individuals, groups or teams, we approach a task thinking it will be 'a piece of cake'. There are occasions when that isn't the case, and frustration and annoyance arise. Many situations *have* no easy answer. The problem posed by this exercise may be solved quite quickly, or it may take rather longer, in which case such negative feelings may be evident. Any discussion needs to look at these.

This exercise also highlights the difference between group work and teamwork. So far it has been assumed that you accept the desirability of teamwork. Some discussion should however recognise the more negative aspects of teams once they have been established and have gained confidence in themselves: Such disadvantages include:

- making life difficult for new members
- restricting entry for new ideas if they threaten the status quo ('groupthink')
- restricting changes when members are happy with the status quo.
- being overly competitive

Some people are uncomfortable when the competitive spirit ventures above the surface. The sporting analogy with teams is therefore problematic when co-operative group work is involved: team members on the face of things may be co-operating, but only to be better competitors.

It is worth bearing in mind that good teamwork enables everyone to be a winner!

Comment

'A group which works as a team can consistently and flexibly out-think and out-perform any one of its individual members. A group which cannot work as a team will consistently and predictably sabotage all but a few of the gifts which each member has to offer, finding it difficult to cope with all but the most routine of problems.' Derby University (1990).

Solution - for those teams in dire straits! For the order in which the pieces fit together, clockwise, take every fifth number in the sequence below, which is deliberately printed upside down to minimise the possibility of seeing the solution before you need to.

43751425846182753863172364871531278263428615

Getting things done! 14

NB: This is a powerful exercise and may bring out strong feelings

Purpose: To aid reflection on different kinds of behaviour in the team

Time: Exercise: 30 minutes
Debriefing: 30 minutes

Materials: A copy of the 'Getting things done! Worksheet' for each team member

Preparation: Photocopy sufficient copies of the 'Getting things done! Worksheet' to have one for each team member

Exercise

1 Appoint two observers and give each of them a copy of the 'Getting things done! Worksheet'.

2 Explain that this exercise is about looking at the patterns of behaviour which occur in all teams. The observers are there so that the rest of the team can participate as naturally as possible, as it is virtually impossible to observe yourself.

3 Explain to the team that they are to imagine that they have decided to go on an outing together. Ask them to plan the outing, and tell them that they *must* come to a conclusion about the following: date, time and activity, eg meal, day at the seaside, etc. The outing needs to take into account the real-life commitments of the team members.

Now, debrief the exercise using the accompanying notes as a guide.

Getting things done! Worksheet

Every team has jobs to do. The football team has to train and play in matches, the admin team has umpteen office jobs to fulfil, the team of mechanics for an airline is responsible for servicing the planes, and so on. The way in which the members of the team get on with each other will affect the achievement of the jobs. So we have divided all this into two main, distinct, but interdependent aspects of the *process* by which the tasks get done:

task:	anything which the team comes together to achieve
maintenance:	the building up and nurturing of the relationships between all members of the team, and in some cases, between other people and teams who are part of the same set-up (company, department, club and so on).

If the *task* is concentrated upon at the expense of looking after relationships in the team, then the co-operation necessary for completing the task does not develop, and the task will not be completed satisfactorily. This in itself causes dissatisfaction and stress.

If the *maintenance* of relationships is concentrated upon at the expense of the task, the achievement of the task will suffer setbacks, people lose motivation and have a sense of frustration. In a workplace, the task sometimes does get completed to the management's satisfaction because the workers need the money and they may be afraid of losing their job if targets are not met. This is obviously not a satisfactory state of affairs from the point of view of the workers in the team - although in some cases the workers may not be aware of the consequences of the unnecessary stress for months or even years. The burn-out rate in some areas of employment is distressingly high.

The kind of behaviour associated with these two aspects is as follows:

Task-orientated behaviour

- **Activism**

  Getting the job done, making sure your own part in the process is fulfilled properly, not wasting time on seemingly irrelevant discussion.

- **Proposing**

  Initiating ideas, suggestions, courses of action relevant to the task.

- **Seeking information**

  Asking for facts, opinions or clarification from other members of the team.

- **Giving information**

  Offering facts, opinions or clarification concerning the task.

Maintenance-orientated behaviour

- **Encouraging**

  Being warm, friendly or supportive of others by verbal and non-verbal means.

- **Gatekeeping**

  Lowering barriers by positively attempting to involve others in any activity concerning the task or the maintenance of relationships.

  Making barriers by excluding, cutting off or frustrating others in any activity concerning the task or the maintenance of relationships.

- **Harmonising**

  Being prepared to compromise and actively accommodate others in order to preserve harmony in the team.

Task-orientated behaviours are 'getting the job done' behaviours.

Maintenance orientated behaviours are 'looking after people' behaviours.

In order to get the job done and satisfy members, a healthy team keeps a balance.

1. Discuss how many of the team, including themselves, showed the following during the discussion:

a) annoyance or *frustration* that having to deal with this issue was stopping the team from doing the jobs in hand
b) a desire to sort the issue out so that if anyone is as *fault* they can be dealt with
c) a desire to sort the issue out so that any problems in *relationships* can be addressed
d) a desire to *help* anyone who may have been at fault over the issue.

2. Give each person (except the observers) a copy of the 'Getting things done! Worksheet' and ask them to spend a few minutes reading through it.

3. Discuss the exercise in the light of this.

Comment

You probably noticed familiar patterns in the way people behaved during the exercise.

Do you want to change any of these patterns, eg if you are always the person who puts difficult issues 'on the table' for the team, do you want to alter this? Exercise No 3 'House rules', (p. 56), may be useful if you want to take this idea further.

'It is a great nuisance that knowledge can only be acquired by hard work' (Somerset Maugham).

Team communication* 15

***NB:** This exercise is adapted from 'Jigsaw' (Arunson, 1989)

Purpose: To improve communication in the team

Time: Exercise: 3 minutes x number in team (maximum 8)
Debriefing: 45 minutes

Materials: Photocopy of Story Sheet (see next page). Paper and pens for each member. Copy of Story Quiz for leader.

Preparation: Cut Story Sheet into 8 pieces as indicated.

Exercise

1. If there are more than eight members of the team, choose eight to take part in the exercise and appoint the rest as Observers.

2. Give one of the 8 pieces of the Story Sheet to each person in the team. If there are less than eight, give an extra piece of the Story Sheet to as many members as needed.

3. Ask each member to write their name at the top of the piece they have been given, and then read and memorise the part of the story on their sheet, *without conferring* with any other participant in the exercise or any Observer. Explain that they have five minutes to do this.

4. Now collect in the Story Sheets and ask each participant to meet every other participant, *one at a time*, to share their parts of the story with each other. Participants may write down notes about the story as they proceed. If any person wants a recap on their part of the story, tell them that they must ask you for their piece of paper, which they must consult *on their own* (no conferring!)

5. Re-form as a team and start the Story Quiz. Give each member a sheet of paper and a pen and ask them to write their name on it and write down the answer to each question as you read them out. At the end, ask each member to pass their paper to the person on their left for marking, and read out the answers.

Now: debrief the exercise using the accompanying notes as a guide.

Story sheet Preparation: photocopy this and cut it into the eight sections indicated

Name ________________ **1**

Mrs Smythe felt miserable. She had just bought a green dress at Clotheswise, and when she arrived home she found that it had a hole in the sleeve near the elbow. She decided to take it back there and then and put her coat back on and went out to catch a No 210 bus back to town.

Name ________________ **2**

On the bus she met an old friend, Mr Singh, and sat chatting to him about various things. Eventually she mentioned that she was on her way back to the shop in Belford to change the green dress she had bought, because she had found that it had a hole in the sleeve.

Name ________________ **3**

Her friend looked surprised, and pointed out that the bus went to Cannington, not to the destination she wanted. She was very surprised and annoyed and realised that in being so concerned about the problem with the item of clothing, she had boarded the wrong bus.

Name ________________ **4**

She hurriedly got up and went down to have a word with the driver. He pointed out that she mustn't talk to him while the bus was in motion. She became flustered and as she turned round to go back to her seat, the bus braked sharply because a dog had run into the road.

Name ________________ **5**

She was thrown sideways and fell down banging her head on a seat. She went dizzy and collapsed. The bus ground to a halt when a passenger told the driver about the accident. A motorist behind in a Ford Fiesta failed to stop in time and ran into the back of the bus.

Name ________________ **6**

An off-duty policeman was passing in his car and stopped to attend the accident. Mrs Smythe was still unconscious and was taken to hospital. The motorist who ran into the back of the bus was breathalysed, and Selford's garage came along to tow away the car and the bus.

Name ________________ **7**

When Mrs Smythe came to in hospital, the police asked her what had happened. She said she couldn't remember much about the incident, except that she hit her head on something. She said that she had a very bad headache and hoped they would leave questioning her till later.

Name ________________ **8**

The motorist who ran into the back of the bus was fined £100 for driving without due care and attention. The owner of the dog which caused the accident was fined £50 for letting it run loose. Mrs Smythe had to stay in hospital overnight for observation.

Story Quiz	Answers
1. How much was the motorist fined for driving without due care and attention?	£100
2. At which shop did Mrs Smythe buy the dress?	Clotheswise
3. Did Mrs Smythe talk to the bus driver when she shouldn't have done, before or after the Ford Fiesta ran into the bus?	Before
4. What symptom did Mrs Smythe have when she recovered consciousness in hospital?	Very bad headache
5. What happened to the bus after the accident?	It was towed away
6. What was the name of the friend she met on the bus?	Mr Singh
7. When Mrs Smythe was on the wrong bus, where was it going to?	Cannington
8. Mrs Smythe bought the dress in which town?	Belford
9. How did Mrs Smythe feel about the dress?	Miserable
10. Why did the bus brake sharply?	A dog ran into the road
11. Which happened first: Mrs Smythe boarding the wrong bus, or the dog running into the road?	Mrs Smythe boarding the wrong bus
12. How much was the owner of the dog fined?	£50
13. Was the policeman on duty or off duty?	Off duty
14. When the motorist ran into the back of the bus, was it before or after Mrs Smythe went to catch a 210 bus?	After
15. What was wrong with the dress?	The sleeve had a hole in it
16. Could Mrs Smythe clearly remember the details of her accident?	No

1. Check to what extent pairs of members found it easy or difficult to concentrate on two things in the same encounter: a) conveying their part of the story to another person, and b) listening to and remembering, and/or making notes about, the part of the story told to them by the other person.

2. How clear was each person in their communication. Communication is a complex process and involves the ability of the person communicating material to express it in an easily understandable form, and it also involves the ability of the person on the receiving end really to listen properly - and as a child once put it 'to want to hear'.

3. To a large extent, this exercise focusses on verbal communication. It is important to remember that this aspect of communication represents only about 10 per cent of the total, the rest being in non-verbal communication, eg posture, gestures, facial expression and colour.

NB: If any members queried the fact that this exercise relied to some extent on memory, point out that members were allowed to recap by looking at their part of the story when they needed to.

Comment

'..... the roles that people take in a team are seldom evident from their features or general appearance. A person making a creative suggestion may look very much like one supplying information. A readiness to engage in dialogue is barely distinguishable from someone trying to take charge. With so much visual noise about, the correct signals cannot be read with any confidence.

That is why when a group of strangers meet for a purpose so much time is spent in probing, in weighing up each other and avoiding getting down to real business. It may even be argued that such 'wasted time' is well spent; for in the course of these personal interactions, preliminary manoeuvres allow perception to be formed. From these, basic relationships can be established. Such a seemingly profligate use of time may in reality serve to increase the prospects of success.'

Belbin (1993)*

*The authors regret that no page number is available for the above quotation.

Crises, hazards and obstacles

Exercises about things which may get in the way and how to deal with them

Crises, hazards and obstacles

Moving the roadblock 16

NB: This exercise is specifically designed for a team feeling 'stuck'.

Purpose: To help team members to understand and solve their teamwork problems

Time: Exercise: 30 mins
Debriefing: 30 mins

Materials: A copy of Roadblocks for everyone

Preparation: Photocopy sufficient copies of Roadblocks (on the next page) for each person to have one

Exercise

1. Give each member of the team a copy of Roadblocks.

2. Ask members to work individually and prioritise the list of common experiences, given on Roadblocks, which may describe the team's problem as seen from the individual's point of view (1 for the one that's most true for the individual, 2 for the next one and so on).

3. Work through the responses, giving each team member a chance to read their answers. The team will need to find a way of collating or recording everything on a flipchart.

4. Discuss the picture which has emerged. Come to an agreement about 1 - 3 points which seem the most important.

Now: debrief the exercise using the accompanying notes as a guide.

Roadblocks

___ I feel unable to make the most of my time, energy and skills

___ I am not sure about what this teams wants of me

___ I do not feel that my personal goals and attitudes fit in here

___ I feel that I lack the attitude and ability to rise to new challenges and opportunities

___ I do not seem to have the ability to generate sufficient new ideas

___ I do not feel that anyone takes any notice of what I say, and decisions are made without me

___ I feel that the leader does not get the best out of me *(This one is risky, don't duck it).*

___ I do not feel that I work together well with my fellow team members

All teams get stuck at times. This is not surprising, given the complicated number of relationships generated by even a small team.

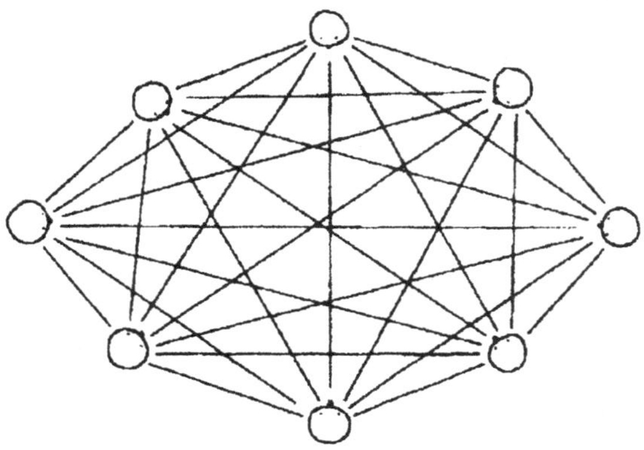

In a group of only 8 people there are 28 relationships going on at any given time!

Reproduced from *Once upon a group*, p. 10

Belbin (1993)*, a notable writer on teamwork, suggested that:

> ..... unbalanced teams with the poorest records fell into two categories. Either they failed completely to read the signs, and carried on as though they were a team without problems; or they recognised the problems early on but acted fatalistically as though unable to change their fixed destiny.

The trap is pretending that problems do not exist or that they will go away. Unchecked, teamwork problems drastically interfere with 'productivity', so it is worth investing the time in working for change.

It does not need to be like this. Just as a good diagnosis is vital to the treatment of a medical problem, accurate assessment makes the difference here. Taking an analogy from holistic medicine: your treatment is within your own power.

You have made a diagnosis by doing the exercise - the hardest part! Moving the road-block will take longer. The following may help:

* The authors regret that no page number is available for the above quotation.

Ways of trying to remove or diminish barriers

Ask each person concerned to write down, on their own, under the following headings, what they would like to say to anyone else in the team:

- Please do the following things, which would help me to be more effective
- Please continue to do the following things you already do, which help my effectiveness
- Please don't do the following things, or do them less often

These suggestions are then exchanged and used a as a basis for trying to resolve the problems.

The exercise on valuing each other in the final part of this workbook may also help.

Comment

If this has been a difficult exercise, it is worth noting that it could be a 'dangerous opportunity'. We all seek balance and calm in our social and working groups. Upsetting this balance can lead to a turning point. Finally, we believe that, however stuck and intractable a situation may be, the 'many heads are better than one' idea *always* works.

> Ideally, teamwork involves the definition of common goals and the development of a plan to which each member makes a different but complementary contribution (Payne 1982, p. 13).

Building bridges - almost literally! 17

Purpose: To develop the problem-solving ability of teams

Time: Exercise: 15 mins
Debriefing: number in team x 5 mins - eg 10 in team = 50 mins

Materials: For each three members of the team: 2 pieces of wood about 2.5cm (1") thick - other dimension doesn't matter. 2 sheets of A4 paper, minimum 80gsm (eg normal photocopier paper).
a 500gm tin of food.
For the leader: a ruler calibrated in inches as well as centimetres.

Preparation: None specific

There are teams who are not satisfied with the given problem!

Exercise

1. Form the team into groups of three. If there are any people left over, make one or more groups four in each. Ask each group to go to a different part of the room with their materials, and to position themselves so that, if possible, they cannot easily see what other groups are doing. If the room has tables, the exercise can be done around these, otherwise groups will have to use the floor (which can be a bit back-breaking!)

2. Ask each group to place the pieces of wood so that the depth measurement is 2.5cm (1 inch) and the pieces are parallel approx 230mm (9 inches) apart.

3. Explain that they must use one of the pieces of paper in some creative way so that they can support the tin of food at least 2.5cm (1 inch) above the working surface between the two pieces of wood. The other piece of paper is for experimentation. The tin must not be supported on the pieces of wood. No scissors, rulers, pencils or any other equipment may be used - only bare hands and the piece of paper!

Now: debrief the exercise using the accompanying notes as a guide.

1. Let each group in turn:

a) demonstrate any results they achieved
b) describe how they approached the problem - what ideas did they try, and which were discarded? What thoughts went through their minds?
c) describe any feelings they had:
- when they knew what the exercise was about
- while they were doing the exercise
- when they had finished

2. Demonstrate the following solution if none of the groups has solved the problem satisfactorily:

- Tear off a strip about 25mm (1 inch) wide from long side of paper.
- Take the remaining large piece and concertina fold it so that the folds run the length of the sheet. The folds should be about 10mm (0.5 inch) apart. NB: All folds must be carefully done to give maximum strength to them. Take care in any of the above not to destroy the natural strength of the paper by badly made creases.
- Now tear the 25mm strip in two, to make two pieces about150mm (6 inches long). Make tears in each piece as shown by the dotted lines in the diagram.

- Wrap each strip round the concertina piece as shown in the diagram and secure by inserting one tear into the other. The strips stop the folds spreading when the tin is placed on it.

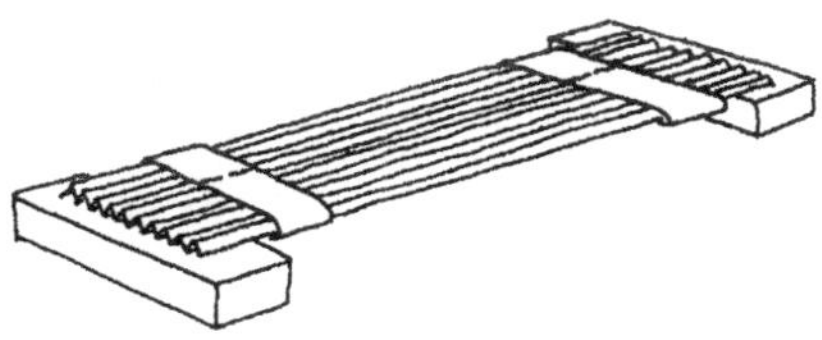

3. Ask each group in turn to share with the other groups their degree of creativity as individuals and as a team when they were engaged in trying to solve the problem.

Optional: Ask each group in turn to share with the other groups the quality of the team-work they experienced when they were engaged in trying to solve the problem.

Comment

Maslow (1973) says that there are three types of creativity:

- Primary creativity is concerned with processes similar to dream formation, the generation of symbolic images, myth, legend, ritual and fantasy. It is more concerned with content than form, with metaphor than structure.

- Secondary creativity is concerned more with structure and with developing original solutions to problems, designing rather than dreaming.

- Integrated creativity incorporates the above two types.

This exercise invites people to develop original solutions to problems, and in so doing they will be experiencing primary, secondary and integrated creativity.

'A person's mind, once stretched by an idea, never returns to its original shape.'*

*The authors regret that no reference is available for this quotation.

The crunch! 18

Purpose: To examine how crisis or 'crunch' incidents in the team may be handled

Time: Exercise: 45 minutes
Debriefing: 45 minutes

Materials: Copy of Crunch Sheet (see next page) for each member. Flip Chart and marker pens.

Preparation: Make copies of Crunch Sheet for each person

This exercise is adapted from a standard exercise which cannot be located in its original form. The authors are indebted to its creator.

Exercise

1. Give each member a copy of the Crunch Sheet and ask them to fill it in.

2. Form the group into pairs, joining one yourself if there is an odd number.

3. Ask one member in the pair to share what they have written in *Part 1 only* of their sheet with the other member, asking them to say how they would have responded to the crunch experience. Tell them that when this has been done they should discuss the suggested responses in relation to what the first person wrote in *Part 2*. Explain that after this they are to reverse the roles so that the second person has a turn with their 'crunch' experience.

4. Now ask the pairs to get together again as a team. Ask each person, in turn, to read out Part 1 of their Crunch Sheet, and then ask the team to choose one of the 'crunch' experiences on which to focus. The person whose experience is chosen, reads out *Part 1 only*, and members, in turn, say what they might have done to resolve the situation in a helpful way for those involved.

5. When each member has had their turn, the chosen person says what he/she actually said and/or did.

Now: debrief the exercise using the accompanying notes as a guide.

Crunch Sheet

Part 1

In the box on the right, make notes about **the context only**, **not mentioning names**, of a recent incident in which you were involved, in which you felt upset, frightened, very anxious or embarrassed.

In this box don't say how you responded in the situation.

The incident can have taken place with one or more other people, and may have happened in a work, social or home life situation.

Part 2

In this box write down how you actually responded to the situation, what you thought, and how you felt.

Part 3

In this box, say whether or not you were satisfied at the time with your response, and if not, whether you had thoughts afterwards about how you may have responded differently.

1. Ask the team to reflect on the response made by the chosen person and the responses suggested by the rest of the team. These reflections could include consideration of the following:

In relation to the chosen crunch experience:

• Was sufficient information given on which the rest of the team could base their suggested responses?

• What feelings were aroused in the chosen person and the other person or persons involved, and how were they dealt with?

• What roles were knowingly or unknowingly being played by the people involved.

• Did there appear to be any ‘hidden agendas’ being played out by those involved.

• At what point did things *start* to go wrong, and where did they *mainly* go wrong, and what could have been done to retrieve the situation at these points?

• Were there any responses by anyone involved which helped to escalate the problems?

• Were there any responses by anyone involved which helped to alleviate the problems?

• What kind and quality of communication, including non-verbal, was evident?

• What levels of stress seemed to be around in those involved?

• What do you think the chosen person learned from being involved in the incident?

In relation to the responses given by the team:

• To what extent were the responses clear or vague?

• What roles were knowingly or unknowingly being played by team members during the exercise? Eg, was anyone mentally sitting in judgement?

• How did team members deal with any feelings which were around, in particular:
  - anger
  - aggression
  - envy
  - jealousy

• Did there appear to be any ‘hidden agendas’ being played out by team members during the exercise?

• Did any manipulation take place?

• Were there any responses by team members which were helpful to the person who related the crunch experience?

• Were there any responses by team members which were unhelpful to the person who related the crunch experience?

• Did the team learn anything about self-assertion from discussing the incident, and the responses by those involved in it, and the responses during the exercise?

Comment

There has been much research on how people react in ‘crunch’ situations. Your emotional state is vital in governing any interactions. McDermott and O’Connor (1996, pp. 42-43) say the following:

To have more choice about your emotional state, identify ..... what sights, sounds, tastes, smells and touches put you in an unresourceful or negative state? (Irritation, hostility, depression, feeling helpless, harassed or fearful are examples of unresourceful states). Sad states ar not necessarily unresourceful. Is your trigger a particular tone of voice? A particular facial expression? The sound of rain first thing in the morning? A full in-tray?

When you notice the trigger you have taken a significant step towards breaking its hold. Start by pacing yourself. Pay attention to how you feel. 'Do in *need* to feel this way?' 'Do I *want* to feel this way?

When you find yourself in an unresourceful state, simply stay with it in an interested way. Pace yourself. Notice which parts of your body are involved in it and which are not. Being with the state in this way can cause it to change and evolve. You may feel tired and feel like relaxing for a few minutes. You may feel renewed energy. Your state will change once you give it attention.

States organise your physiology in a characteristic way. Changing physiology changes state. This may be why *pretending* to be happy can actually have real physical effects. Changing thinking will not work unless it brings a shift in physiology - whether deliberate or involuntary is irrelevant.

Food for thought!

Your needs or the team's 19

Purpose: To sort out the difference between behaviour which satisfies personal or team needs

Time: Exercise: 45 minutes
Debriefing: 15 minutes

Materials: Pen and paper for each person. A copy of 'Self oriented behaviour' for each person

Preparation: Photocopy enough copies of 'Self oriented behaviour' (next page) for each person have one

Exercise

1. Give a copy of 'Self oriented behaviour' to each person and ask them to spend a few minutes reading and digesting it.

2. Ask members to think of an instance when they have exhibited one of the listed behaviours when in the team. Ask them to be honest! Then ask them to write a few sentences which describe the incident. Tell them *not* to justify their behaviour.

3. Now ask people, in turn, to read what they have written.

4. If anyone cannot think of an instance of any of the behaviours, see if others agree with them. It should be an interesting discussion.

5. Work out how far each of the behaviours met the individual's or the team's needs.

Now: Debrief the exercise using the accompanying notes as a guide.

Self oriented behaviour: Kakabadse et al (1988)*

Attacking/defending	• Attacking or rejecting others, or defensively strengthening one's own position.
Blocking/stating difficulties	• Placing blocks or difficulties in the path of others' proposals or ideas without offering an alternative proposal or reasoned argument
Diverting	• Moving the discussion away from areas in which you feel your position is threatened or weak.
Seeking sympathy/recognition	• Attempting to make others sorry for you, and therefore willing to support you, or actively attempting to gain positive feedback on the value of your contribution to the group process.
Withdrawing	• Refusing to make a contribution
Point scoring	• Seeking to score points off other members to enhance your status.
Over-contributing	• Monopolising discussion in the group, using the group process to satisfy individual power and control needs.
Trivialising/diluting	• Picking on minor points of discrepancy in others' proposals or contributions in order to determine their positions.

* The authors regret that no page number is available for the above.

This may have been a heated or uncomfortable discussion. As with all the exercises, our contention is that it is worth unpicking the everyday occurrences, so that people have the chance to reflect on their ways of operating, and make changes if necessary. No one can be blamed for *unconscious* behaviour. It is what we do when people point it out that matters. Take time to allow people to take on difficult feedback, and return to the exercise at a later date.

Comment

> It is sometimes difficult to see the difference between maintenance oriented behaviour and self oriented behaviour; the same behaviour may be displayed, but the motive for this behaviour, eg gate-opening or closing, may be either to maintain group harmony or to satisfy personal needs.
>
> Kakabadse 1988*

* The authors regret that no page number is available for the above quotation.

Assess the stress 20

Purpose: To assess the levels of unacceptable stress in your team

Time: Exercise: 30 mins
Debriefing: 30 mins

Materials: 1 copy of Assess the stress Worksheets 1 & 2 and 1 sheet of A4 paper per team member. Flip chart and marker pens

Preparation: Make a copy of Assess the Stress Worksheets 1 & 2 (next 2 pages) for each team member

Exercise

1. Give each member of the team a copy of the Assess the Stress sheet, pen and paper and ask them to follow the instructions. Make it clear that the worksheets are *confidential, ie not to be shared within the team,* unless anyone wishes to share anything from them.

2. Ask if anyone would like to share anything from their Worksheets and their list, and if appropriate, write it on the flip chart

Now: debrief the exercise using the accompanying notes as a guide.

Assess the Stress - Worksheet 1

Note: This sheet is personal and not to be shared within the team

Assess your personal level of unacceptable stress (Adapted from Evans and Pottage 1994*)

Circle the level at which you experience each symptom.

0 = symptom experienced not at all   5 = symptom experienced very often

Important: *on Worksheets 1 and 2 are some of the main symptoms of unacceptable stress. They can also indicate physical and mental conditions other than those caused by stress. If one symptom is experienced very often or several symptoms are experienced at the same time, then you may need to take medical advice to determine the cause and treatment.*

Physical symptom	**Not at all**					**Very often**
Difficulty in sleeping	0	1	2	3	4	5
Feeling constantly very tired	0	1	2	3	4	5
Easily startled	0	1	2	3	4	5
Getting out of breath easily	0	1	2	3	4	5
Nail-biting	0	1	2	3	4	5
Fast pulse on slight exertion	0	1	2	3	4	5
Sighing deeply	0	1	2	3	4	5
Poor appetite	0	1	2	3	4	5
Indigestion or heartburn	0	1	2	3	4	5
Comfort eating	0	1	2	3	4	5
Crying or feeling like crying	0	1	2	3	4	5
Sweating without any exertion	0	1	2	3	4	5
Headaches	0	1	2	3	4	5
High blood pressure	0	1	2	3	4	5
Constipation or diarrhoea	0	1	2	3	4	5
Nervous 'tics'	0	1	2	3	4	5
Feeling sick/nauseous	0	1	2	3	4	5
Dizziness or fainting	0	1	2	3	4	5
Impotence or frigidity	0	1	2	3	4	5
Fidgeting	0	1	2	3	4	5
Unable to sit still for long	0	1	2	3	4	5
Cramps and muscle spasms	0	1	2	3	4	5
Getting a lot of minor infections	0	1	2	3	4	5

Now add up your scores for Worksheet 1: _____

*The authors regret that no page number is available for the above quotation.

Assess the Stress - Worksheet 2

Note: This sheet is personal and not to be shared within the team

Mental symptom	**Not at all**					**Very often**
Lack of concentration	0	1	2	3	4	5
Feeling low and miserable	0	1	2	3	4	5
Don't want to get up in a morning	0	1	2	3	4	5
Hating yourself or feeling bad	0	1	2	3	4	5
Overwhelming fear of open or confined spaces	0	1	2	3	4	5
Difficulty in relaxing	0	1	2	3	4	5
Feeling irritable	0	1	2	3	4	5
Lack of interest in people	0	1	2	3	4	5
Feeling people are ignoring you	0	1	2	3	4	5
Finding difficulty in making decisions	0	1	2	3	4	5
Feeling life hasn't much point	0	1	2	3	4	5
Difficulty in finishing one task before starting another	0	1	2	3	4	5
Difficulty in having a laugh	0	1	2	3	4	5
Fear of failure	0	1	2	3	4	5
Disliking your appearance	0	1	2	3	4	5
No interest in the future	0	1	2	3	4	5
Feeling unable to cope	0	1	2	3	4	5
An overwhelming fear of loneliness	0	1	2	3	4	5
Fear of becoming ill	0	1	2	3	4	5
Feeling other people are getting at you	0	1	2	3	4	5
Feeling there's no one you can talk to	0	1	2	3	4	5

Now add up your scores for this Worksheet:
Enter the score for Worksheet 1: ______
Total for Worksheets 1 and 2: ______

2. Now write down briefly, in your own words, as a list, what you find stressful at present. By 'your own words', we mean: try to avoid the kind of phrases which people bandy around, but which cover up the real feelings, eg put 'The boss is a right pain', instead of 'I'm under pressure at the moment'.

If your score for the 44 physical and mental symptoms is getting close to 15, then maybe you need to alter your life style a little. If it's 15 - 30, then you need to take stock and find some coping strategies. If it's over 30, then life must be rather grim, and you need to take action quickly.

Most of us have a certain amount of acceptable stress in our lives - it's what makes us tick, adds a bit of spice to life, and helps to get jobs done. What is not good news is the unacceptable amount of stress which a lot of people encounter. This can be bad for us, physically and mentally.

As a team, discuss ways of:

a) eliminating as far as possible the factors which are causing unacceptable stress
b) coping better with the factors which cannot be eliminated, which are causing the unacceptable stress

Coping with stress

- **Early warning system** - Every so often use the Assess the Stress sheets to find out your current state of physical and mental health.
- **Lifestyle** - change this where possible - find out the causes of your unnecessary stress and try to reduce or eliminate them.
- **Diet** - Plenty of fresh vegetables and fruit, and cut down on sugar and salt.
- **Drink** - Plenty of water, some fruit juices and keep to the recommended alcohol intake - 21 units per week for men, 14 for women.
- **Caffeine** - keep intake to a minimum. Remember that as well as tea and coffee, chocolate contains caffeine!
- **Exercise** - Regular exercise is very good for helping people cope with stress. Choose exercise which is suitable for you - and if it's fun as well, you are more likely to keep it up. If in doubt about what is suitable, ask your doctor.
- **Sleep** - Try to establish regular bedtimes and do winding-down things before you go to bed, like watching or listening to comforting or humorous programmes, and having a relaxing warm bath. Regular exercise will help to promote better sleep.
- **Drugs** - try not to use smoking as a way of reducing the effects of unhealthy stress, and avoid non-prescription drugs.
- **Time** - Allocate time for relaxation and leisure. All work and no play .....!
- **Fun and laughter** - Circumstances for some people may make it difficult or impossible to experience any fun and laughter in their lives. If, however, your circumstances permit, try to create opportunities for having some fun - it's a great antidote to stress. 'Laughter is the best medicine'.

Most people have things happening in their lives outside of the life of the team, which adversely affect their performance in the team. Addressing these in any depth is outside the scope of this book, and anyone who feels that their performance is being adversely affected should consult a doctor, counsellor or psychotherapist.

Comment

Teams need to 'create a stress barrier from the demands of the outside world' (Morrison 1986, p. 26).

Helping the team after a stressful event 21

Purpose: To facilitate team support after a stressful event, such as a fire, an attack on someone, or a serious accident

Time: Exercise: 2.5 hours including debriefing

Materials: Flip chart and marker pens

Preparation: Arrange a comfortable room where members will not be interrupted for 2.5 hours. Organise refreshments. Find out where your nearest Post-Traumatic Stress centre is located. Find out if your organisation has any specialist service available for debriefing, and ask for a facilitator to help you, if so. Find out and obtain leaflets or contact numbers of support organisations, eg Victim Support. Read the debriefing notes and make copies of them for members.

NB: This exercise needs to take place 48 hours to one week after the stressful event. It is helpful, though not essential, to have someone from outside who has experience in leading such groups, as facilitator, for the exercise.

Introduction

1. Explain that the team has been through a stressful experience and that it can be helpful to talk through the event using a particular format. Explain that this is not therapy or counselling, it is a way of helping the team to move on.

2. Stress the need for confidentiality. It may be that there is a need for representation or feedback to be given to someone outside the team, and the content of this needs to be agreed by all.

3. Say that it is important that there are no interruptions. Mobile phones definitely off!

4. Explain that you are going to work to a particular format which has been found helpful in these kinds of situations.

5. Reassure members that they are not going to be 'put on the spot', blame is not going to be apportioned, and that they need not speak, and can stop speaking at any time they wish.

6. Say that the team will decide upon what feedback will be given to anyone outside, eg managers, as a result of the meeting.

7. Say that it will be helpful to keep to the following structure, not in order to deny people their right to speak, but to gain maximum benefit from the session.

Exercise

Try not to rush any of the following stages.

1. Ask each member to describe what they remember of the event, not for accuracy, but for how it *felt* to them individually.

2. Now ask members, in turn, to supply *information* with as many facts as possible, so that as full a picture as possible is constructed of what happened.

3. Ask each member to describe their first *thought* when the stressful event took place.

4. Ask each member to describe their *strongest* feeling when the event took place.

5. Ask each member to describe the *worst* aspect of the event for them, then and now.

6. Describe common reactions to stressful events and reassure that these are *very common*, and that such normal reactions include:

- being unable to sleep
- nightmares
- 'flashbacks' or distressing reminders of the event which keep intruding on the mind
- feeling it was your fault
- feeling that others suffered more or less than you
- constant fear that it will happen again
- avoiding everyday things which remind you of the event

7. Give information about what to do if the reactions they have described are still at a distressing level after 3 months:
   - visit GP
   - contact Post-Traumatic Centre, if one is available
   - contact any local organisations offering support which have been found

8. Ask team members to list the things they can do to support each other.

9. List any things which the team would like to discuss with the wider organisation, if it is part of one.

10. Give out debriefing notes

12. End with refreshments.

Now: debrief the exercise using the accompanying notes as a guide.

Comment

Debriefing was an integral part of the exercise in this case. However, you may be interested in the following:

The exercise has been derived from the work of Mitchell (1983) and others, around the reactions which people have to stressful events. These have been conventionally thought of as disasters, such as the Bradford football stadium fire, but members of teams are also affected by violence from service users, accidents, or witnessing distressing scenes on a daily basis. The effects can be cumulative; ie an individual fireman may have apparently coped successfully with a hundred fires, and seemingly inexplicably go to pieces after the hundred and first.

Human beings have instinctively known that sharing their reactions with each other helps. This includes the discussion during tea break or the chat on the journey home. In recent years workplaces are under so much pressure that the time and opportunity for informal debriefing is frequently not there. So the *organised* debrief may be necessary.

Mitchell and others found that remarkably good results follow from supportive intervention (within 24-48 hours is ideal) and that the effectiveness decreases with time. 'After six weeks the effectiveness is minimal and team members are more vulnerable to lifelong emotional fallout'. (Mitchell 1983, p. 37).

The Consequences of Traumatic Stress

Immediate consequences of trauma, affecting the majority of people who experience severe stress, include:

• Emotional symptoms: shock, intense fear, tearfulness, anger, shame, helplessness, nervousness, numbness.

• Mental symptoms: confusion, disorientation, unwanted memories, decreased concentration.

• Physical symptoms: bodily injury, muscular tension, fatigue, edginess, change in sleep and appetite, gastro-intestinal problems, racing heart, bodily aches and pains.

Long term consequences of severe stress can be complex and severe, including marked interpersonal changes such as apathy, anger, and isolation; and psychiatric disorders such as:

• Post-Traumatic Stress Disorder (PTSD): re-experiencing the trauma in memories and dreams, avoiding anything reminiscent of the event, memory loss, emotional numbing, sleep disturbance, anxiety.

• Depression: loss of hope, self-worth, motivation or purpose in life; fatigue, decreased pleasure in previously enjoyed activities, changes in sleep and appetite, suicidal thoughts or actions.

• Alcohol and substance abuse.

Treatment

> While the consequences of traumatic stress are severe and complex, treatments are available that significantly reduce symptoms and improve quality of life.
>
> Trauma After Care Trust (2000, p. 5).

Two national centres of help if symptoms do not decrease after three months:

Trauma After Care Trust (TACT) Helpline: 0800 169 6814

The Nottingham Trent University Centre for Traumatic Stress, Research and Practice: 0115 941 8418

Celebrating progress

Exercises for valuing ourselves and our team

Celebrating progress

22 Only me
23 Team versus individual performance
24 Straight aim!
25 Our value

Team versus individual performance 22

NB: a minimum of four people is required for this exercise, and six or more is ideal.

Purpose: To demonstrate that tasks are more effectively carried out by teams than by a set of individuals

Time: Exercise: 20 minutes
Debriefing: 30 minutes

Materials: A copy of the printed quiz (next page) - or your own quiz for each member - kept secret by the exercise leader

Preparation: Find at least 2 rooms to work in; make a copy of the printed quiz for each person (or devise your own quiz and make the necessary copies).

Exercise

1. Divide the team into two equally sized groups. (If you have 12 or more people you could have three groups). Ask each group to wait in a separate room.

2. Give each individual member of all the groups a copy of the questions, and tell them that they are not allowed to look at them until you say.

3. Tell the members of one of the groups that when you give the signal to start, they are to complete the quiz as individuals, without speaking or communicating in any other way.

4. Tell the members of the other groups that when you give the signal to start, they are to complete the quiz as a group, producing one set of answers.

5. Tell all those taking part in the quiz that the time limit is 15 minutes, give the signal to start, and at the end of it call the groups together.

6. Read out the answers and ask the individuals and the group(s) to add up their marks.

7. Compare results.

Now: debrief the exercise using the accompanying notes as a guide.

You have 15 minutes in which to try to answer as many of the following questions as you can. Write the answers in the spaces provided. There is 1 point for each correct answer making a possible total of 20 points in all.

Q No

Solve these anagrams:

1.	CONE:	_ _ _ _
2.	NIGHT:	_ _ _ _ _
3.	LANCED:	_ _ _ _ _ _
4.	ANYTIME:	_ _ _ _ _ _ _
5.	INTEGERS:	_ _ _ _ _ _ _ _
6.	ARGENTINE:	_ _ _ _ _ _ _ _ _

Which number comes next in each series?

7. 1, 2, 4, 8, 16, 32, __
8. 0, 1, 1, 2, 3, 5, 8, __
9. 1, 2, 4, 7, 11, 16, __

Which letter comes next in each series?

10. O, T, T, F, F, S, S, E, __
11. J, F, M, A, M, J, __

Could the following square fit inside the circle without touching it?
The square has sides 5cm long. The circle has a circumference of 21 cm.

12. Tick one: YES ___ NO ___

What letters do you get from the following?

13.	The last letter of the name for an alloy of copper and zinc	__
14.	The letter immediately left of 'V' on an English typewriter keyboard	__
15.	The 1st letter of the other name for the incus bone in the ear	__
16.	The 2nd letter of the colour between blue and yellow in a rainbow	__
17.	The 9th letter of the capital of Mexico	__
18.	The last letter of the surname of the winner of the men's singles final at Wimbledon in 2001	__

In Britain nowadays, in terms of length of time:

19. Which is the shortest month of the year? ____________
20. Which is the longest month of the year? ____________

Answers

1. **ONCE**
2. **THING**
3. **LANCED**
4. **AMENITY**
5. **STEERING**
6. **TANGERINE**

7. **64** (each number is twice the previous one).
8. **13** (each number, after the first two, is formed by adding the previous two together, and is a recognised series in mathematics called the Fibonacci series).
9 **22** (the difference between adjacent numbers increases by one).

10. **N** (the letters are the initial letters of the numbers one to eight, so N for nine is next).
11. **J** (the letters are the initial letters of the months of the year from January to June, so J for July is next).

12. **No** (in order to fit inside the square, the length of the diagonal of the square would have to be less than the diameter of the circle. The length of the diagonal can be calculated by using Pythagoras theorem which says that the square of the length of the hypotenuse of a right angled triangle is equal to the sum of the squares of the lengths of the other two sides. So 5 squared plus 5 squared = 25 + 25 = 50. The square root of 50 is just over 7 as 7 squared = 49. The way to find the diameter of a circle when the circumference is known is to divide the circumference by 'pi'. As pi is approximately 22 divided by 7, the diameter of 21 multiplied by 7 and divided by 22 comes to less than 7. Therefore the square will not fit inside the circle.

13.	**S**	Last letter of BRASS
14.	**C**	
15.	**A**	1st letter of ANVIL
16.	**R**	2nd letter of GREEN
17.	**T**	9th letter of MEXICO CITY
18.	**C**	Last letter of IVANISEVIC

19. **February** (It has 28 days, or 29 in a leap year, and every other month is longer).
20. **October** (The clocks are put pack in October making the month one hour longer than the other three months which have 31 days)

How were your results? We dare to predict that the team did better. You may argue that this is self-evident, but you may not have done all the exercises in earlier sections, hence this one.

The exercise works on the principle that pooling skills gets better results than when people work as individuals. There are many more complicated versions of this exercise, but the principle always works, unless the numbers are so low as to make the distinction between an individual and a team almost meaningless.

Check how the individuals in the isolated group are feeling. Another positive aspect of teamwork is that it does not leave people feeling alone or that they are in competition. The exercise may have raised some of these feelings.

Comment

This exercise has been put first in this section so that you will be confident in the ability of teams to do better than individuals. Obviously, this depends on the activity: composing music or painting pictures are usually, but not always, individual pursuits. However, it is interesting that , in recent years, some scripts for television drama series have been written by teams. Isabel Briggs Myers*, whose work has given some inspiration to this book, said that she dreamed that her work would go on helping people to value their differences rather than using these to destroy each other.

**Myers-Briggs Type Indicator*™ and MBTI™ are trademarks of Consulting Psychologists Press, Inc.

Only me 23

NB: This exercise is especially useful for multi-function teams.

Purpose: To help members of teams to value each other

Time: Exercise: 10 mins
Debriefing: 30 mins

Materials: 1 sheet of paper and a pen/ pencil for each person

Preparation: None specific

Exercise

1. Ask everyone to think about all the different kinds of jobs which are done by the members of the team either as individuals or in co-operation with other members. Now ask each person, on their own, to write down the kinds of jobs which only they can do. (Allow 10 minutes for this).

   Note: This is not whether the person is *capable* of doing it.

   Example: Often there is only one person in an organisation who is authorised to sign for expenditure.

Now: debrief the exercise using the accompanying notes as a guide.

1. Choose someone to start by reading one of the jobs on the list they have just made. Ask the person to say why they think that only they can do that job, and then ask the other members of the team whether or not they think this is a fair assessment.

2. Repeat the process with each person in turn, and then, as necessary repeat the process for the second jobs, then the third and so on until all the jobs on all the lists have been discussed, as in 1 above.

Comment

There is usually very little that can be done only by one person. This tends to de-mystify certain jobs which are regarded as the most expert. On the other hand, the authors have had the experience over and over that people who describe themselves as 'only the caretaker' or 'only the secretary', are vital to the team. If the operating room floor is dirty, the surgeon's skill will certainly be wasted if the patient gets an infection.

There is normally little that the team can do about the pay and conditions of 'ancillary' staff, but there is much that can be done about giving them their true worth in other ways.

To a certain extent, the authors believe that 'the character chooses the job'. This is not to dismiss the lack of choice which many people have due to injustices in society. However, as Goldsmith and Wharton (1993, p. 86) put it:

> There is a Yorkshire phrase 'There's nowt so queer as folk', which is just another way of expressing astonishment at the rich diversity of personality types that we see around us. All different, and yet with sufficient common strands for us to be able to recognize that certain types seem to belong together. There is a strange tension in groups of people which seems to need opposites, contrasts or complementarities in order to maintain the equilibrium of our social fabric. We need each other, and even people we find difficult to understand or appreciate have an important role to play in ensuring that all the gifts are shared out, that all the skills are available, and that each one of us has a special place and part to play in the overall scheme of things.

Straight aim! 24

Purpose: To recognise your straight aims

Time: Exercise: 45 mins
Debriefing: 30 mins

Materials: Copy of Aims Sheet per person. Flip chart and pen

Preparation: Make a copy of the Aims Sheet for each person

Exercise

1. Give each member of the team Aims Sheet and ask them to spend 10 minutes filling it in on their own.

2 After the 10 minutes is up, form pairs for 10 minutes to try to reach agreement about the team's achievements.

3. Come together as a whole team and try to reach agreement about the sheet as a whole and record the results on a flip chart.

Now: debrief the exercise using the accompanying notes as a guide.

Aims Sheet

Spend 10 minutes on your own completing these statements from the point of view of *your own* understanding of the team. You should have completed the relevant assessment exercises in 'Where are you now?' before doing the exercise of which this sheet is part.

Our main aim as a team should be ______________________________

____

____

____

We do the following things well: ______________________________

____

____

____

The best things about being in this team are: ______________________________

____

____

____

If we were to advertise for a new member, we would highlight: ______________________________

____

____

____

1. Discuss the following:

- What factors influenced members in deciding on responses to the Aims section? How much was concerned with the team's needs, how much was to do with individual needs? Were there any 'axes being ground'?

- In reflecting on what the team does well, how far was success in doing the task a factor, and how far were harmonious relationships important to you?

- Was a great deal of concern expressed about how people outside the team should be treated, or was there a feeling that all that mattered was how the team functioned?

- What were your priorities in choosing a new member?

Do these reflect something you feel the team lacks? Could this be supplied if everyone's skills were more fully utilised?

Comment

Curiously enough, many teams do not spend enough time recognising their strengths and valuing themselves. This could be because the work ethic in the industrialised countries has rubbed off even in voluntary activities: emphasis on blame, productivity and targets.

It can be useful to move away from this by describing the preferred future, a technique used by counsellors in brief therapy. Ask yourselves:

- what would I like to be different when I next meet the team?

- who will be the first person to notice any changes?

- what will he/she see?

We believe that you have the ability as a team to straighten these aims if they have gone a little off course.

Our value 25

NB: This is a deceptively powerful exercise

Purpose: To help team members to value each other

Time: Exercise: 3 mins x number of team members
Debriefing: 5 mins x number of team members

Materials: Flip chart and marker pens. Pens. A pad of 'Post-its'. An envelope marked with each person's name

Preparation: None specific

Exercise

1. Give out a pen and enough 'Post-its' for each member to use one for each member of the team. Ask everyone to write down the qualities which they value in *each* of the other team members, using one Post-it for each team member. Ask them to be 'specific'. Example: 'X is very supportive' is non-specific, whereas 'X always makes a drink for people when they are down' *is* specific. They can be signed or not.

2. Ask members to 'post' the comments in each of the envelopes and then hand out the envelopes.

3. Give people time to read the comments in their envelopes. A break and a drink is useful here.

4. Optional: Put the Post-its on a flip chart, grouping each member by name.

Now: debrief the exercise using the accompanying notes as a guide.

1. Give each person a chance to say something about the contents of their envelope.

2. Discuss the following:

- faults in others often rise to the fore in teamwork
- it is easy to see, and/or imagine faults in ourselves, if we have a low sense of self worth
- it is important to be, or become, aware of our own worth, to value ourselves, and to be aware of the qualities which are of value in ourselves
- it is important to be, or become, aware the value of others, and to be aware of the qualities in them which are of value
- feedback is best if it is specific, not general. If yours wasn't, see if you can ask team members to tell you what they meant.

3. Our experience is that many people find it very hard to hear positive things about themselves and that tears are just as common as when criticism is given. An exercise like this can really lift someone's sense of value - a sad comment on our society that this does not happen more often! Were there many surprises for you and other team members? Were you seen in the same way by most or did you receive a variety of compliments?

A final comment

The book ends at its beginning, with an emphasis on the things which can be missed when the going gets difficult - as we said - it's a journey!

> We shall not cease from exploration
> And the end of our exploring
> Will be to arrive where we started
> And know the place again for the first time
>
> Eliot (1958)

References

ARUNSON, 1989. Jigsaw. **Simulation/games for Learning,** 1991, 21 (2) 191.

BARANICH, K., 1992. The role of gender in the design of computer-based training games. **Simulation/Games for Learning,** 22 (3), 153-161.

BELBIN, R. M., 1981. **Management teams - why they succeed or fail.** London: Heinemann.

BELBIN, R. M., 1993. **Team roles at work.** Oxford: Butterworth-Heinemann.

BERNE, E., 1976. **Games people play.** London: Penguin.

BERNE, E., 1976. **Using the Myers Briggs type indicator in organisations: a resource book.** USA: Consulting Psychologists' Press.

CRYER, J., 1990. Games people play in educational games, simulations and workshops: a transactional analysis perspective. **Simulation/games for learning,** 1990, 20 (4) 368-377.

DERBY UNIVERSITY, 1990. **Trust in team building.** Derby: unpublished.

EVANS, M. and POTTAGE, D., 1994. **The competent workplace.** London: NISW.

GOLDSMITH, M. and KINDRED, M., 2001. **Developing Teamwork ... from an understanding of personality.** Southwell: 4M Publications.

GOLDSMITH, M. and WHARTON, M., 1993. **Knowing me - knowing you.** London: SPCK.

HIRSCH, S., 1985. **Using the Myers-Briggs type indicator in organizations: a resource book.** Consulting Psychologists Press, Inc.

HOFFMAN, L., 1993. **Exchanging voices: a collaborative approach to family therapy.** London: Karnac.

HONEY, P., 1983. Learning styles - their relevance to training courses. **Training Officer,** 1983, 108-110.

HONEY, P., and MUMFORD, A., 1986, 2nd Ed. **The manual of learning styles.** Maidenhead: Peter Honey.

HUNT, J., 1979. **Managing people at work.** London: McGraw Hill.

JACQUES, D., 1984. **Learning in groups.** London: Croom Helm.

KAKABADSE, A., et al, 1988. **Working in organisations.** London: Penguin.

KINDRED, M., and KINDRED, M. 1998, New ed. **Once upon a group.** Southwell: 4M Publications.

KINDRED, M., and KINDRED, M. 1998a. **Once upon a group exercises.** Southwell: 4M Publications.

KNOWLES, M., 1983. Androgogy: an emerging technology for adult learning. **In: M. TIGHT,** ed., **Adult learning in education.** Chicago: Croom Helm.

McDERMOTT, T, and O'CONNOR, J., 1996. **Neuro-linguistic programming and health.** London: Thorsons.

MASLOW, A. H., 1943. A theory of human motivation. **Psychological Review**, 50, 370-396.

MASLOW, A. H., 1973. **The farther reaches of human nature.** Harmondsworth: Penguin.

MITCHELL, J., 1983. When disaster strikes. **Jems**. January 1983, 36-39

MORRISON, T., 1986. Beyond the sum of its individuals. **Community Care,** September 4th 1986, 26-28.

NATIONAL INSTITUTE FOR SOCIAL WORK TRAINING, 1996. Leadership, teamwork and changing practice. **NISW Noticeboard,** 19, November 1996.

PAYNE, M., 1982. **Working in teams.** London: Macmillan.

SCHUTZ, W. C., 1958. **FIRO: a three dimensional theory of interpersonal behavior.** New York: Holt, Rinehart and Winston.

TRAUMA AFTER CARE TRUST (TACT), 2000. Tact matters, Sept 2000, 1-7.